Limestone pavement at Winskill

In memory of our Grandparents

George and Jeanne Butler
Mary and Jim Bradley

First published in 2013 by Watching Sparrows Publications.
1 Wisp Hill Croft, Moody Sty Lane, Grassington, BD23 5NG
www.watchingsparrows.co.uk

www.workingtheview.co.uk

ISBN 978-0-9576052-0-6

Designed by studioFOLD

Printed in Belgium by DeckersSnoeck

Working the View

Yorkshire Dales National Park

Mark Butler & Sarah Butler

Introduction

We often take the landscape around us for granted. We might appreciate a view for its beauty, but not think to consider the natural and historical processes, or the everyday work and care that goes into managing and sustaining it. *Working The View* explores this relationship between the landscape of the Yorkshire Dales National Park and its guardians; bringing to light the work that goes on to protect, enhance and make a living from it.

This book is the result of a brother and sister collaboration between photographer Mark and writer Sarah. It features 40 participants who have shared the stories behind their favourite views. Each person was asked to suggest three viewpoints which have specific meaning for them. From these, a broad spread of locations was selected from throughout the National Park and its potential extension to the north and west.

Mark spent a year and a half photographing these views, often returning to the same areas again and again to ensure each view was captured in the best season and light conditions available.

Sarah interviewed each participant to discover the reasons behind their choice and learn about the work they do in the landscape. Each interview was recorded and then written up into a coherent 'piece', using the words of the participants. As a result each interview reads as if spoken and retains the 'voice' of the participant.

We could never hope to showcase every voice and every role in the National Park, but we have brought together a range of individuals; from farmers and landowners, to people employed by organisations working to protect the landscape. The result is a unique tour of the National Park area, given by the people who make the landscape what it is today and who are working to ensure it is protected into the future.

Working the View is supported by the National Lottery through Arts Council England.

Key

15 Approximate image location and direction

Yorkshire Dales National Park boundary

Potential extension to the Yourkshire Dales National Park

Contains Ordnance Survey data © Crown copyright and database right 2013

1. **Whernside from Ingleborough**
   chosen by Steve Hastie, Area Ranger, Yorkshire Dales National Park Authority
2. **Threshfield Moor**
   chosen by Mark Hancock, Landowner
3. **Ingleborough from Twisleton Scar End**
   chosen by Louise Smith, Lead Adviser, Land Management, Natural England
4. **Wild Boar Fell at dawn**
   chosen by Matt Neale, Area Ranger, Yorkshire Dales National Park Authority
5. **View over Cray**
   chosen by Peter Katic, Ranger, National Trust
6. **Wensleydale from above Castle Bolton**
   chosen by Richard Spensley, Farmer and Landowner
7. **Widdale Great Tarn**
   chosen by Jane Le Cocq, Farm Conservation Adviser, Yorkshire Dales National Park Authority
8. **Moughton Scar**
   chosen by David Sharrod, Director, Yorkshire Dales Millennium Trust
9. **Calton fields**
   chosen by Robert Crisp, Farmer
10. **Barden Moor**
    chosen by Paul Wilby, Headkeeper, Bolton Abbey and Chatsworth Estates
11. **View towards Simon's Seat**
    chosen by Phil Richards, Area Ranger, Yorkshire Dales National Park Authority
12. **Pecca Falls, Kingsdale Beck**
    chosen by Alistair Nash, Site Manager, Woodland Trust
13. **Nethergill from Oughtershaw Moss**
    chosen by Fiona Clark, Farmer, Nethergill Farm
14. **Halton Gill**
    chosen by Katherine Wood, Principal Planning Officer, Yorkshire Dales National Park Authority
15. **View from Fountains Fell**
    chosen by Tony Bullough, Ranger, National Trust
16. **Smardale Gill from Witches Stride**
    chosen by Andrew Walter, Reserves Officer, Cumbria Wildlife Trust
17. **View from above Dent**
    chosen by Margaret Taylor, Farmer, High Laning Farm
18. **Juniper Gill, Moughton**
    chosen by Fran Graham, Wildlife Conservation Officer, Yorkshire Dales National Park Authority
19. **Austwick from edge of Oxenber Wood**
    chosen by Gail Smith, Community Worker, People and the DALES, Yorkshire Dales Millennium Trust
20. **Booze Moor**
    chosen by Ceri Katz, Peatland Restoration Officer, Yorkshire Wildlife Trust
21. **Kilnsey Trout Farm**
    chosen by Anthony Roberts, Landowner

22. **Dawn mist from Conistone Pie**
chosen by Geoff Garrett, Senior Trees and Woodlands Officer, Yorkshire Dales National Park Authority

23. **Askrigg and Addlebrough**
chosen by Allen Kirkbride, Farmer

24. **View into Coverdale**
chosen by Gary Verity, Chief Executive, Welcome to Yorkshire and Sheep Farmer

25. **Booze ruin**
chosen by Miles Johnson, Countryside Archaeological Adviser, Yorkshire Dales National Park Authority

26. **View from Cautley Crag**
chosen by Alison O'Neill, Farmer, Shacklabank Farm

27. **Hawkswick dawn**
chosen by Roger Gibson, Drystone Waller, Fencer and Landscape Contractor

28. **Langcliffe Brow**
chosen by Dave Tayler, Deputy Director, Yorkshire Dales Millennium Trust

29. **Howgill Fells**
chosen by David Butterworth, Chief Executive, Yorkshire Dales National Park Authority

30. **Pen-y-Ghent from Gorbeck**
chosen by Gary Lodge, Farmer, Westside Farm

31. **Valley of Desolation waterfall**
chosen by Roy Lingard, Head Forester, Bolton Abbey and Chatsworth Estates

32. **Dentdale from Spice Gill**
chosen by Kevin Milburn, Farmer

33. **Ingleborough in winter**
chosen by Carl Lis, Chair of the Yorkshire Dales National Park Authority

34. **View over Ravenseat**
chosen by Amanda Owen, Shepherdess, Ravenseat Farm

35. **Mallerstang Edge ruin**
chosen by Annie Hamilton-Gibney, Community Archaeology Project Development Officer

36. **View from Stags Fell**
chosen by Tessa Levens, Peatland Restoration Officer, Yorkshire Wildlife Trust

37. **Howgill Fells from above Raisbeck**
chosen by Jan Hicks, Textile Artist and Smallholder

38. **Upper Wharfedale from Moor End**
chosen by Martin Davies, Countryside Property Manager, National Trust

39. **Coverdale from Flamstone Pin**
chosen by Dave Higgins, Project Manager, Yorkshire Dales Rivers Trust

40. **Sunset from Addlebrough**
chosen by Roger Gaynor, Dales Volunteer, Yorkshire Dales National Park Authority

41. **Grassington sunset**
chosen by Sarah Butler, Writer

42. **Muker from Kisdon Scar**
chosen by Mark Butler, Photographer

Steve Hastie

Area Ranger / Project Manager Three Peaks, Yorkshire Dales National Park Authority

I used to do short term contracts for English Nature before I came to the Yorkshire Dales National Park Authority. I was doing estate work on the nature reserve, so things like walling repairs, fencing repairs, thistle control, ragwort control. I was always up on Ingleborough, so I kept seeing this view of Whernside. Whernside from most angles isn't particularly spectacular. From the north it's just like a big lump, but as you go up Ingleborough it starts to take on a bit of a character. And as you come further round onto the summit, that view twists again and it looks like a bit of a peak. It's a false impression: you're actually looking along the edge of that scar where it falls away. So it's not the actual peak you're looking at but it gives the impression of it.

This view of Whernside reminds me of a gentle swell coming into a beach, just before it starts to rise and turn. I can almost imagine it moving, which is quite a strange thing for a hill, but in my mind that's how it's got most character.

It's taken from High Lot – a large allotment that belongs to Natural England. It's allotted land, and a lot of Ingleborough is common land as well. Ingleborough Common is split into two, between Ingleton and Clapham – there are Ingleton graziers and there are Clapham graziers, and they each have rights to graze so many sheep and cattle over the course of a year. A lot of this area has been overgrazed, subsequent to the Second World War, but heather's starting to come back now the grazing's under management. This field used to be quite rough grassland, but now there are these little patches of heather; it sort of breaks it up.

The path runs just to the left of here. It's part of the Three Peaks network. As well as Area Ranger, I'm Project Manager for the Three Peaks Project. It's the second project of that name. The first one was in the 1980s and '90s; that was about doing a lot of path construction and habitat restoration work to provide some sort of sustainable network. It was the worst network in the UK at that time. With this peat, when it gets worn it gets really soft, and then water gets in it and scours it, so people walk off to the side, and it just gets worse and worse, and paths get wider and wider. Lots of work was done building paths, so people had something decent to walk on, and by building paths it allowed the surrounding vegetation to recover. In 2008 we started looking at a second project to raise money to get another person to do maintenance work, to make the network sustainable. So we look at engaging with people who come and use the area, to try and encourage them to help us look after it, essentially through some sort of donation or giving.

As Area Ranger, a third of my time is woodlands and species; a third of my time is communities – which could be anything from speaking to a local councillor, a farmer, a WI group; a third of my time is access; and then a third of my time is the Three Peaks Project! It's very varied, very satisfying.

Mark Hancock

Landowner

There are about 1000 acres of moorland at Threshfield. It's predominantly heather, and we're doing a huge amount of work at the moment to improve its habitat and environment. There are only 459 heather moors in the UK, which amount to 75% of the world's heather, so it's an endangered species in a way. We need to protect this environment in order for a range of birdlife to survive and thrive. Predominantly these are ground nesting birds including grouse; you can't breed them, you just create the right habitat for them. Carrying out this heather regeneration work to create a productive grouse moor has enabled us to create employment for two gamekeepers. Rural employment is a big issue for me. Without it, more and more young people will move away from the countryside.

I've lived in the Dales for 16 years. For a time my wife was Chief Executive of the National Park, so we have a strong affinity to the area. We bought this land off a good friend of mine in 2009. He bought the moor in 1961 and looked after and enjoyed it for 48 years. I have another moor in Littondale and he really liked what we were doing there in terms of regeneration. He offered me the chance to buy the land in order to keep the spirit and the philosophy of the moor intact, and in tune with the way he's been looking after it for all those years. So I'm endeavouring to do that.

My background is in commercial property development, but rural regeneration has become one of my passions because of where I live. We've just brought back to life some beautiful barns just outside Settle on the A65 which we have called The Courtyard, with retail units on the ground floor and a Brasserie on the first floor. We've created 25 new jobs, and the food production that's going on up on the moor here will feed into the restaurant, as well as into the pub we have brought back to life near where I live. Locally sourced and produced food is also really important to me.

I chose this view because there's a bit of rarity in having the water in the picture. It's a predominantly limestone-based environment, so we rarely see standing water. I also love the fact that at any time of day, in whatever weather, you get the reflection of the sky.

The biggest residential cluster in the area is Grassington; I particularly love this view because while you don't see Grassington you know it's there. So although we're in a wilderness up here, there's a tangible connection with cars and people and bustle and shops. I think that one of the things the National Park was set up to create in 1947 was to allow people to enjoy themselves and come to the Park. It's not a closed space – we want people to live and to work in the Park; we want visitors to come because we want the shops to thrive and people to succeed. But if it's done overtly we tend to frown upon it because we get honeypots like those in the Lakes. Here, we know it's all going on and yet it's absolutely not getting in the way at all. It's that perfect balance between allowing society to function without spoiling the countryside. For me personally, it makes that view across there very special.

Louise Smith

Lead Adviser, Land Management, Natural England

I've worked in this area for about 11 years now. When I came up here I didn't know anything about the Dales. I'd moved up from Staffordshire and Hereford, which is a very different type of landscape. From day one Ingleborough just stood out. It was always my main route coming along the A65, out of Leeds, or the Lakes; making my way back to the Dales I would see this iconic shape on the horizon – it just always made me feel like I was back where I wanted to be.

Over the years of working up here, I've worked in the farming and wildlife team for the National Park. I've worked on the Limestone Country Project which covered a lot of the European designated areas, which Ingleborough is part of. I'm now back with Natural England, as a lead adviser working on environmental stewardship. I couldn't believe my luck when they put me back in this area – I could have been sent anywhere. It was as if I was meant to be here; this place kept bringing me back.

It doesn't matter whether the sun's shining, it's tipping down with rain, or Ingleborough's got snow on it; that hill, even if it was covered in cloud, would still be amazing. It reminds me of my years working here and all the characters that have shaped it in their own way.

The characters that make this landscape living and breathing are the farmers, the farmers' wives, anybody that lives in that area; they are part of that landscape. They have such admiration for it, and you can't help but have admiration for them wanting to preserve and work on such a beautiful landscape. I think I've grown by working with them and learning from them, which I feel very privileged to have done.

The area's so diverse, it was one of the hardest places to get into the correct management. It's a delicate balance between the farming side and what we want to see for the environment and nature. We tried to achieve the correct balance through experience gained from other areas but mostly by stopping and listening to people that know this site. The people that you really listen to are the people that work this site every day, and that's the farmers. Of course they need this hillside. They utilise the more green in-bye areas when they're lambing, but later on in the year they need their sheep to push up onto the hillside, because they need to shut their meadows so that they can cut the hay. It also makes their stock hardy, but more importantly it completes the unique upland farming cycle that helps shape this precious landscape.

This whole area, the Yorkshire Dales, is like one big family. Yes, some of the time you have to work a little bit harder to be accepted. But as soon as you know that you're on the same common ground; the same wavelength; and you're not there to preach at them and tell them to change their ways; you're in partnership with those people because you have the same aims, then boy oh boy that door's open then. You can be in one of the most remote dales that you can get, in some of the bleakest weather, but you never worry because you know that if something ever happened, you could just walk down that farm track and knock on that door and somebody would be there to welcome you.

By working with different farmers, particularly round Ingleborough or Chapel-le-dale, you'd find these secret nooks and crannies on this hillside – areas where you just think, 'crikey, I bet nobody's been up here for years'. You could be on your own for hours and you wouldn't feel lonesome, you'd just feel as if you're in another world. I know I make it sound so romantic, but there's never a day when you're out on that site, or you're looking at that view, from any direction, that you don't have a smile on your face. Honestly, you can have the worst day in the office and once you get out there it's forgotten.

Matt Neale

Area Ranger, Yorkshire Dales National Park Authority

This is on one of my local runs. I get the train up to Kirkby Stephen early in the morning, run over Wild Boar Fell and back home, which is about 12 miles. I do it in all weathers: in the light and in the dark, on my own or with a couple of us. I experience it in all sorts of weather conditions and light, and there's just my own feelings that go with that: whether I'm struggling on the run or actually going really well – that all adds to the atmosphere up in that area. Even though I've been over there quite a lot, sometimes it just makes you stop and look, and think 'this is incredible'.

I do a lot of mountain, or ultra-distance running. I've done quite a few hundred-milers. What I like about them is that you experience all the dark and all the light of a 24-hour period, and you just feel really in touch with what's happening in the environment. That's quite a big thing.

This area is actually outside of the National Park at the moment. It's been decided that this, and a larger area to the north and to the west of it, qualifies to be designated as National Park, so in the next few years I'm sure that will happen. That view is more or less looking into the National Park. It's a really nice area. It's great looking down into this bit of the Mallerstang valley: you've got the road; you've got the railway line; you've got the source of the River Eden and the River Ure. It's a big dividing point for a lot of things. You get views over onto the Howgills; and a really good view of this big massif of land at the top of Wensleydale; the top of Dentdale, and if you like the top of Horton. You can pick out the Three Peaks on a good day.

Of course you've got these piles of stones – there are a few trains of thought as to why they may or not be there. There's a theory that they were built to appear like soldiers on horseback if you're standing in the valley bottom and looking to launch a bit of an attack. They're just nice features really, however they got there and whatever the reason behind it.

I'm the Area Ranger for Upper Wensleydale. I spend a lot of my time dealing with access related issues, so primarily that's to do with people's enjoyment of the rights of way network. In Upper Wensleydale there are about 150 miles of rights of way that I have to look after. I manage an Access Ranger who helps do that, and I get a bit more involved in the legal issues.

The rest of the time, we're very much a first point of contact for the rest of the Authority, and we play quite a big part in getting volunteers out and managing volunteers, not just for us but across the Authority. I'm working quite closely with our wildlife conservation team at the moment on a red squirrel project. We've got a small population of red squirrels in this area, and it's just taking a bit of sensitive management. It's quite a critical time for the red squirrel population here at the moment; it's right on the borderline of being a sustainable population. I've no doubt that in some areas of England red squirrels will get lost over the next 10 or 15 years, and it's nice to think that we have the chance to do our bit for one of our native species. It would be nice, even if it doesn't work out here, to be able to turn round and say 'well, we did the best we could with what we had'.

You do have to be a little bit brutal sometimes. If you're not careful, you could let email and everybody else's urgent demands start to take over. What you've got to remember is that you haven't got rights of way, or woodlands, or red squirrels emailing you to say 'come and spend some time sorting out our problems'.

Peter Katic

Ranger, National Trust

As you're coming from the north, from Bishopdale over Kidstone's pass, this is the first view of Wharfedale you get; it's really dramatic. You see Buckden Pike on your left, with these enclosure walls tumbling down the hillside towards Cray. On the other side of the valley you've got a similar sort of landscape, but the fields are all hay meadows, not pasture.

The reason I work for the National Trust up here, in this type of property, is that I like the uplands. I like the open space, the open vistas, the ability to walk a long way with no obstructions, the fact you can see where you're going, the wild aspect of it. In as much as you have wild landscapes in this country, this is a wild landscape, even though it's totally manmade, and very accessible; everything you see is farmland.

The drystone walls emphasise the wild aspect of the landscape; they draw out the rock that's there, only just underneath the surface. They bring out that stepped aspect of the landscape too, the geology of what's called the Yoredale Series, which is a repeating sequence of limestone, sandstone, shale. You can see quite distinct terraces, with steeper slopes in between and occasional rock outcrops. People think that's manmade, but it's not, it's a glacial relic if you like, from the different hardnesses of the rock.

Being a Ranger means doing a lot of practical work: footpath maintenance, fencing, tree-planting, making individual tree guards, woodland creation, wall repair. Walling hasn't changed much; it's a link to the past, an ancient craft. It's been around for thousands of years, just using materials that are around.

This little plantation you can see down in Cray was probably planted in the 1800s. It's all non-native species – beech trees, sycamore, maple and scotts pine. Maybe it was planted for shelter, maybe because it softens the landscape a bit. We rebuilt this wall on the right, where you can see the saplings, with the help of a group of regular volunteers. It was completely gappy, and falling down. We rebuilt it so we could put in a strip of trees between the road wall and that wall. The Dales is an open landscape, with very few trees – and perhaps we don't want to change that aspect too much – but if we can get a long strip of trees here it sort of breaks up the wind and gives the farmer's livestock a bit of shelter.

Another feature of the Yorkshire Dales is the limestone pavement. You can see a small example of it in the foreground here. When the ice retreated after the Ice Age, it left these bare platforms of limestone. Limestone dissolves in rainwater, so over thousands of years the minute cracks you get in limestone enlarge, and what was at one time just a smooth bed of rock breaks into blocks which are called clints. The cracks are called grykes; they can be ten feet or more deep. Within the grykes you get a more woodland type of environment, with damp, shade-loving plants like hearts-tongue fern and meadow sweet. It's like a little mini-woodland growing in the gryke. On the clints you get a more limestone habitat – with grasses, rock rose, and wild thyme.

My father was Serbian. He lived in a limestone area in Croatia. That landscape's much bigger and more rugged than this one, but there are similarities. If you walk between Yockenthwaite and Scar House, it has a feel of the landscape that he comes from. His family would have lived in that area for generations - you wonder if a love of one kind of landscape can be in the blood.

Richard Spensley

Farmer and Landowner

This view's my life in a nutshell. I was born at Aysgarth; my family's farmed here for 150 years. How I visualise it is that the heart of Wensleydale is here. You have the arteries running off it, which are Walden, Bishopdale and the top end of Wensleydale. They come together at Aysgarth and you get this wide expanse of fertility. Further down dale it opens out and levels, but this to me has always been the heart of the dale.

That's my land in the foreground. We bought 1146 acres of which my daughter had 200, my son has sort of 900, and grazing rights on 2005 acres of heather moor. My son farms the major farm – basically this building and all this land in front. My daughter, they're on a rented farm but they have the best bit of land that's out of sight here.

The bottom of the dale here's always been dairy, but it's significantly changing now, in that there's only one dairy farm in sight from here. Every householder used to have a cow – these little buildings are all for two cows. The village here was an old mining village. 60 working people lived in this village – there are only 30 houses now. Majority had a field, a field house as we know them, and right to graze in two big pastures behind.

Farming at the moment in these dales and the upper dales is totally dependent on brown envelopes as we call them – handouts of one kind or another; environmental schemes. They have a place, the money's required, but if the agriculture was viable on its own, the environment would have been sustained in a satisfactory manner without the money. Before, the only expense virtually was man hours – two horses if you liked and fodder for your cows, which you grew. But that now doesn't create a living wage. This farm in the '40s and '50s was carrying seven hired men. The farm now carries one hired man and my son, and they have an increased sheep flock and an increased cattle herd. The sheep flock will be 10% higher, the production off that will be 30% higher, and cattle

will be 200% higher. Before, if you were milking 40 cows in that area, 100 gallons of milk was a large farm. When my son-in-law left he had 13-1400 gallon a day going off the same land.

The sheep areas are to a large degree totally dependent on the environmental payments. The lamb production off the uplands, whilst it's always going to be beneficial to the environment and the sustainability of the visual aspect, is very difficult to sustain financially without outward assistance.

We've planted trees in that gully you can see through the Millennium Trust. It's waste land to a degree, nothing but rabbits and rocks and elm skeletons. We've put in a standard mix of a lot of wild cherry, and we've included some scots pine – which aren't on the Millennium Trust menu, but are advantageous to black grouse. We've actually had black grouse in there. We lost them a couple of winters back with the frost. They're quite rare round here.

It is a pleasurable experience doing the work in good weather. I like the achievement of helping the livestock and the land to produce. It's a total encompassment of the whole aspect of living. It's bigger than land. It's the fact as school kids we knew where every bird's nest was from here to school - we knew what there were.

I think the main thing that crops up in my thoughts is how insignificant our lifetime is, on the whole dale. There are things there that'll have been worse than brownfield sites in the mining days, and yet they're grassed over and forgotten. I mean some of these lynchets – the plateaus – from the 8th, 9th, 13th and 14th centuries would have been massive excavations. And then the creation of the mill. And yet there's nothing there. If you study it as an archaeologist you see bits and pieces, but there's no significance.

Jane Le Cocq

Farm Conservation Adviser, Yorkshire Dales National Park Authority

This view is taken from the top of Widdale Fell, with Dent and Garsdale in the distance. This is a farm I was doing a survey on in 2011. It was a hard slog up to the top of Widdale Fell. It was a really clear day and you could see all the Lakeland hills in the distance. I walked across the top of the fell and suddenly came across this fantastic tarn. The water was really, really still, like a millpond, and I just thought, 'Wow!' – it was so unexpected.

The top of Widdale Fell is heath. There was quite a bit of blanket bog: deep peat which supports plants like heather and cotton grass. That was basically what I was going up there to survey. Down here (just behind where the picture's taken) I found the ruins of a little shepherd's hut, which had a tiny fireplace in the corner of it – it was really lovely. It is high up there, and you can just imagine them on a night, huddled round a little fire while it's blowing a gale.

I'm a Farm Conservation Adviser. Part of my job is to help farmers get into Higher Level Stewardship. In order to do that they have to have a survey done of the whole farm. You have to record every feature, whether it's moorlands, meadows, woods, barns, walls – everything. It's all done on foot, with a map, just marking down as you walk everything that's there; the type of habitat; what condition it's in; and what they could do to improve it for various species.

This farm has been in Stewardship for quite a number of years. Before they went into Stewardship there was a lot of exposed peat, and not much heather, possibly due to the number of sheep being grazed. When sheep graze, the heather, cotton grass and other small herbs get eaten out. It's replaced by rough grass, so other species miss out. If the peat's exposed it leads to a lot of erosion, and then you're losing carbon, because peat bogs are a vital carbon sink – comparable to forests even. The environmental schemes help to compensate farmers for reducing or taking stock off those areas.

Now up here the exposed peat is revegetating. There's red and black grouse and other moorland birds, lots of diversity in the sward itself: lots of little herbs and rare bog plants like sundews – which sound boring, but they're not really!

I've always been interested in wildlife and nature. I used to be a veterinary nurse. I lived in the Channel Islands for years, but when we came back to Yorkshire I had to do something different, because the veterinary nursing didn't fit in with family and lifestyle. I retrained, and over quite a few years took a degree in environmental conservation. And then luckily a job came up here, which I got, in 2005.

I grew up in Otley. We had relatives up in the Dales so I knew it really well. I used to be a volunteer here at the Park when I was a teenager - I always dreamt about working in the Dales.

I like everything about my job. I like being able to get out and go to places which you'd normally never get access to. I like the diversity – you do a bit of ecology; a bit of woodland management; I'm really interested in vernacular architecture so that fits in really well too. I like meeting the farmers.

We have a family farm with suckler cows. Because I've got a veterinary nursing background, I do all that type of thing, and also paperwork and admin. I love it. It's also good because in my work I can see things from both sides. My sons are not at all interested in conservation and would be happy with acres and acres of ryegrass!

A lot of my job is trying to illustrate to farmers that they wouldn't necessarily be losing out economically, and in some cases they might be better off in Stewardship, because they know they've got a set income for ten years. And when you show farmers what they've got on their farms in terms of biodiversity and historic features, a lot of them are really interested. Often they haven't seen it in those kinds of terms before – they've just seen it as somewhere to raise livestock. But because the species and habitats wouldn't be there without farmers managing the land for livestock production, it's important that that management carries on.

David Sharrod

Director, Yorkshire Dales Millennium Trust

This is taken on top of Moughton Scar; a ridge that runs sort of midway between Pen-y-Ghent and Ingleborough. Despite being in the middle of one of the most heavily visited and best loved parts of the Dales, not many people know about it.

As you can see, it's limestone pavement. When you stand up there and look towards Ingleborough it's almost a lunar landscape; desolate – in the nicest possible way. I genuinely love it up there. I like it in winter when you've got snow and ice, but also in late summer when you get the contrast between the heather and the limestone.

I've always thought that the best views in high country are actually not from the highest peaks, but from slightly lower ones, whether that's in the Alps, or the Lake District, or the Dales. So on Moughton you look across to Pen-y-Ghent and Ingleborough, and you get a sense of their scale.

When I'm up there, I always think that we live on this small, crowded island, but that when you start walking about Northern England you find there's a lot of nothing, a lot of big open spaces and big skies. And then you get the contrast with the valley, of course. Behind you here is Ribblesdale, which is full of life from the farms, the quarries, and the communities there.

I first came to the Dales on a sixth form field trip to Austwick. It was a magical week, and a week that changed my life. It opened my eyes to the Dales as a fantastic place, but there was also a brilliant teacher who changed my mind about a few things – he persuaded me to go to university for a start. I never dreamed that many years later I'd end up living a few doors away from where we stayed.

That experience comes to mind during discussions about our education and outreach work at the Trust. We talk about whether people need ongoing experiences, and a proper structured Introduction to the countryside, but I actually know that bringing somebody out for a day – or if you can a week – can also change somebody's life. We see that happen all the time.

I've worked at the Trust for 15 years now. We have a very wide remit, but also in a way a narrow remit, which is to support the well-being of this area, as simple as that. We started off with a big Millennium Commission grant, to do a landscape project essentially: tree planting, restoring drystone walls, field barns, historic buildings, historic features, wildlife habitats and community buildings. We've carried on doing landscape work, but we've also diverted into all sorts of other things, because you soon realise that everything in a landscape like this is interconnected.

One of the simple premises of our charity was that 18,000 people live in the Park, but millions of people from all over the world visit here or love it, and if you could just get a pound out of each of them every year you could do a hell of a lot. 48,000 people have donated – much more than a pound each! – and we're still here after 15 years.

One of our most obvious impacts has been through tree planting. There are many reasons to plant trees: it's good for wildlife, carbon sequestration, flood control, and the landscape, but above all it's a mark of confidence in the future. We've helped others to plant more than a million trees since 1997. We don't own land ourselves, but we help to pull the money in, co-ordinate the work, and get trees planted. Our tree dedication scheme is still the main source of our donations.

Robert Crisp

Farmer

To be honest I haven't really got a favourite view as such. I've never really thought that much about it. It's just part of landscape – you take it for granted. I mean, if I go up there tomorrow and there isn't that view, I would know then, but because it's there I just accept it. I go up there every day to feed the sheep in spring. I always find it very relaxing because you're away from everybody; I just find it easy there.

I moved here in 1959 when I was four. My father died when we were in our teens, and me and my brother just kept farming, with my mother at that time. When he died my mother got tenancy. I remember she used to go down to help milk and keep coming back in to get us ready for school. It's just what happens in farming. It's a way of life; it's what we do. We were just 100 acres then. That was quite adequate to make a living off, but you can't make a living off 100 acres any more. Everyone's going at a faster pace these days. It's a bigger scale; you're pushed more. Supermarkets are controlling prices and you're playing with quantity. We need supermarkets, but they've got a lot of power.

We're quite fortunate. There were three farms in this village and this is the only one left. They were sold off in bits, and that's enabled us to expand. A couple of years ago we managed to actually buy the farm. Up until then we were producing milk as well as sheep, but the next generation don't want to be tied to producing milk; you have to be here twice a day. The next generation have seen there's more things out there, and we aren't getting any younger.

I farm with my brother, and I've got a daughter who farms – she goes to New Zealand every winter shearing sheep for about four months. We've got about 300 acres of that kind of land you can see here, and 300 acres of moorland, and just under 1000 sheep. We run a couple of hundred geld hog lambs, which are last year's lambs that are coming into flock next year. They go onto moor because all they've got to do is grow. We put Swaledale sheep with one lamb onto other moor, then we put Swaledale Pures further up. Breeding stock with twins we keep on the better land. It's all fairly good land to be honest. It's quite steep up at the top here, steeper than it looks in this picture.

I don't find farming side stressful, I find paperwork stressful; there's so much paperwork with it these days. But I don't think I'd ever want to do anything else. You're just free, aren't you? When you go up there, you're away from people. You're up there and it's yours, and you're quite privileged really that other people in theory can't be there.

You can't ask for a better way of life to be honest. But after saying that there are downsides. There are some days when you're stuck in a puddle and it's raining or it's windy or it's snowing or whatever, and you think 'why am I doing this?!' We do have problems with people too: they do leave gates open and they do bring dogs. It's quite frustrating when you go up onto moor and see somebody with a dog running about. The sheep naturally run, and when they're carrying two or three lambs they aren't meant to run; you do get abortions. Most people don't understand – they don't know they're in lamb. If they see some lambs there they're more responsible, but it's more important earlier on.

Each sheep's an individual. You sort of recognise them. You keep seeing them and you think, 'oh yeah, that's the one that did whatever last year'. You do – as farmers put it – *ken* sheep. They are different in lots of ways – they look different, and they act different. All right, if you've got a thousand and there's one missing, you can't pinpoint it to 'it's that one missing', but you've a fair idea. It is an interesting way of life.

Paul Wilby

Headkeeper, Bolton Abbey and Chatsworth Estates

Bolton Abbey is the Yorkshire estate of the Duke & Duchess of Devonshire. It covers approximately 30,000 acres in total. 14,000 acres are grouse moor with the River Wharfe running through the middle, creating two almost equal moorland areas east and west of the river.

I was lucky enough to come here to work for the family in 2006. It's a great family to work for; they're really interested and they really care about the moor. I've been in grousekeeping now for over 40 years – virtually all my working life. I actually come from Essex and the moorland here very much reminds me of the marshes – that wildness and that quiet.

Moorland gamekeeping is about maintaining the habitat in a way that suits grouse, and making sure the moor is there for future generations. It's about looking after it in a proper manner, without abusing it, or doing anything to damage it.

When asked for my favourite view, I was tempted to say 'wherever I happen to be looking any time I'm at work'; this is an outstandingly beautiful part of North Yorkshire. The view I have chosen is one from the lunch hut on Thorpe Fell, looking straight down the valley to Strid Wood and Beamsley Beacon on the horizon. You can see the moor's been worked for generations – that's part of its interest. The chimney of the old Onion Hill colliery in the foreground is a monument to all those who worked there. Coal was sledged down to Thorpe village and then taken to Grassington to be used for smelting lead in, I think, the 1700s.

When I was here in the early '70s, this area was partly covered by hundreds of acres of bracken. Its condition now is testament to the determination of the family and staff and the scale of the conservation project they've undertaken.

You can just see black parts here, where we've burnt strips of heather. The patterns created by heather burning are so important for the health of the moor and its wildlife. What we're trying to produce is a mosaic of everything from freshly burnt to long heather, so that the grouse have got nesting cover, shelter, and food in various shapes and forms. We burn it because when it gets old it loses nutritional value – it gets leggy and not very palatable. You also want short heather, and bare ground for the chicks to get out on to dry. One advantage of this is that all the waders like the short heather and the burns too, so you get the curlews and golden plovers coming up to nest, which adds to the diversity of the wildlife. Ideally you want lots of small burns. Grouse are territorial. If they can see each other they'll fight and defend their territory, so the more broken up the ground is the more territories you can have, and that way we can maximize stock levels.

When you're up here, you get the wider panoramic view that takes in Simon's Seat on the left all the way round to Halton Heights on the right. It's a view I never tire of looking at. It's a good place just to stand and enjoy, whether on a spring day with the grouse and curlew calling, in the summer with the heavy scent and colour of the heather, or a still clear cold autumn day. I enjoy being up there in all weathers, just thinking 'this is where I belong'.

Phil Richards

Area Ranger, Yorkshire Dales National Park Authority

I got to pick one view, but I could have picked a dozen easy, of equal quality to that. I never get tired of the Dales landscape. It's a fantastic place to live and work, and it's nice to feel like you're protecting it for the future. I don't think I see it as a job: it's just doing what you feel in your heart. I'm very lucky to be able to do that.

This is a view onto Simon's Seat, taken just opposite Parcival Hall. It's quite prominent, Simon's Seat, as a gritstone outcrop. It's also part of what we call the Barden Moor and Barden Fell access agreement, which allows people to walk not just up to Simon's Seat but anywhere on this open moorland.

It's very much a managed landscape, predominantly for red grouse; however the moorland also offers an ideal habitat for other ground nesting birds such as golden plover, snipe, curlew and merlin.

This is an interesting area because you've got the limestone drystone walls, yet just across the valley you're back into gritstone; there's such a contrast in a very short distance. You've got Trollers Gill just out of shot to the north with lots of limestone crags. Trollers is an old Norse term meaning trolls, not the internet type but mischievous little creatures. Allegedly there's a dog lives up there called the Barguest, which is a Norse mythological large dog. It's a kind of ghost dog that comes out at full moon apparently – so you'll be careful not to go up there.

I'm an Area Ranger. Our main focus is maintaining the rights of way network: building bridges, stiles, putting signposts in, waymarking, gates, and all sorts of things. We've got a big project up on Simon's Seat at the moment, because the peat has got badly eroded up there with people using the paths. We're laying a path using old reclaimed mill flags to create a sustainable route. A lot of them come from Lancashire mills. They weren't just taken off the ground floor; these big flags were maybe four or five levels up – they're massive things. It's quite an interesting concept; when you're up there laying them, you think about all the people who've worked on them and what they were doing.

I've worked here a long time, 20-odd years now. I've probably had four different roles since I started. I enjoy what I do now. A lot of it's management and overseeing work. We've got over 200 volunteers, and part of my role is to support them in undertaking various duties including managing public access on the moorland. Obviously it's nice to get your hands dirty sometimes. I still do some walling, in my spare time, and if something crops up here I'll occasionally pop out and help. It's nice to keep your hand in. And you feel like you've achieved something when you've repaired a wall. You've repaired an all be it man-made landscape, but you've made a difference in a practical way.

Alistair Nash

Site Manager, Woodland Trust

This is Pecca Falls, just above the footbridge on the waterfalls walk in Ingleton. Our part of the woods is on the right hand bank as you're looking at the photograph. From here upwards the falls get progressively bigger, right up to Thornton Falls. I like this view with the water winding off into the distance. It just gives you that taster: you know there's something big at the top.

I've probably been to this wood a hundred times, or more, but every single time it's different. You go in summer and sometimes you can hardly even tell there's a waterfall, there's just a trickle coming down. But if you go after an incessant downpour, you can stand at the bottom of those falls and the whole thing's full of spray and it's just unbelievable – a different place completely. The water's fantastic because it's always this peaty black colour. Even in the middle of summer you can never see the bottom. You've got all this white foam and then it's black underneath.

I could quite happily go up there and just sit for an hour watching what's going on in the water: whether it's a trout in the bottom, or the kingfisher flying up and down, or the wagtail or the heron or whatever it may be – there's always something to have a look at.

I've been the Site Manager there for 17 years now. This is one of the woods that's always been in my portfolio. It's an ancient woodland and Site of Special Scientific Interest, because of the plant life on the limestone and shale; my role's basically protecting that. My job is mainly management: liaising with Natural England, agreeing the work that needs doing, getting all the permissions, and then I've got to organise the contracts, oversee the contractors from start to finish, and undertake all the observations we do on site as part of the management plan. We still have to get out to all the woods during the year, whether it's spot checking on contracts or tree safety checks for the public – there's an enormous list of jobs that go on. I've got 65 sites over five counties, which keeps me very busy.

This wood was 'enriched' by the Victorians. They thought the broadleaf trees weren't interesting enough, so they brought in a lot of other species like larch and spruce. We've been slowly taking those out over the last 17 years, hopefully in a way that doesn't particularly offend or affect anybody in terms of damaging the landscape – that's been quite a delicate task. It's let a lot more light into the canopy and we've got a huge number of ash seedlings coming up in there. We're trying to get it back to as close to what would have been the natural woodland cover as possible.

We've also replaced all the fencing. There were sheep getting in, which had quite a detrimental effect on the ground flora. I've seen the density of the wildflowers increase, and the deer population there has increased quite dramatically over the last few years too.

The prime reason for new planting is to increase the amount of native woodland cover. It's trying to undo what's already been done. In this country we've hammered our woodlands for hundreds and hundreds of years. We've only got about 13% woodland cover, compared to the continent, which has 20 or 30%. We've got a long way to go before we can get back to a reasonable amount.

Obviously the ash dieback that's coming could potentially be a huge issue, because we've been working on getting back to oak and ash woodland since we got the wood. Now we're potentially going to lose three quarters of it. It may be that we need to look at doing other planting on there; we'll just have to wait and see what happens.

I think I've been involved in planting about three quarter of a million trees over my career; trees that I've either planted myself or been the contract manager that's dealt with the planting. That's your mark on the landscape; that's there forever as woodland now.

Fiona Clark

Farmer, Nethergill Farm

This is taken from the Moss, overlooking the farm and Fleet Moss. You can see the three gills – Hazelbank, Chaldron and Mireing. We're called Nethergill, which means 'between the gills'.

The elements are doubled up here. It can be a lovely day in Skipton and then it's gale force up here, torrential rain, and the temperature's just dropped. And yet when it is sunny up here, in spring particularly, it's just magical – that's the only word you can use to describe it.

The majority of our land is this poor, low productivity land, but very rich in species. It's a really fragile environment. People look at it and think it's wild and rugged, but actually it wouldn't take much to destroy it.

You can see our two hay meadows here, the original one behind the house, and a new one at the front; they're both in the Hay Meadow Restoration Scheme. It's creating such a huge increase in biodiversity.

We've planted a new woodland just behind the one you can see in the picture: 30 acres of undulating, fenced in, mixed woodland – 18,500 trees. It's called Ellbeck Wood, after our two daughters – Ella and Becky. We put it in primarily to encourage black grouse, which we've now just got back.

We've just been working on a river restoration project. We're at the headwater, so it rises and falls really, really quickly. As a result of that the banks wear away like mad, just leaving soil, and of course that goes further down and gets into the trout redds and affects them. And of course the flooding in York. It all sort of starts here. You really do feel responsible, because what happens up here has a huge effect down there. So with the Yorkshire Dales Rivers Trust we've been putting willow bundling along the side of the river, and planting willows which will help to keep the otter too.

We have native rare breeds because they're suited to this climate. Whereas this pasture at the front of the picture looks really rough, our native cattle can wander through here and pick out what they need. What we're trying to do is create a balance. We're sort of trying to prove that you can have a hill farm – have native breeds and make that work in terms of selling the special meat off them – but also be kind to the environment and encourage the wildlife as well. It's trying to make the whole thing work together – that's been the aim all the way along. On this land now we've got 11 cows and 100 sheep, which is absolutely nothing really, but that is the stocking rate that creating the right biodiversity demands.

The Higher Level Stewardship scheme is vitally important for us. We run a bed and breakfast. We've just built two self-catering apartments and a Field Centre, which will bring in extra income – we hope. The Field Centre's going to evolve into all sorts of things. We have school groups coming in. It's also open throughout the season, because we're on the Dales Way, so people can just walk in and, with an honesty box, have tea, coffee, chocolate and flapjack. It'll be available for courses. It'll evolve. It's a room we felt we had to have.

This is the sort of project we've wanted to do all our lives. When we took it over it had been on a tenancy agreement for many, many years. The trouble is that when you're renting land the temptation is to take out but not put back in, and not think about the future really. So we were coming to this knowing that everything had been taken from it, but knowing that if we started making changes – even small changes, the changes would be very significant in terms of wildlife. That has actually happened, which is really encouraging. The thing that amazes me most about it is that every little thing we do has such a profound influence on what species are here.

We've been here seven years. It's been a very steep learning curve, and still continues to be. There are lots of steps back, but I think we're going in the right direction.

Katherine Wood

Principal Planning Officer, Yorkshire Dales National Park Authority

This is a view of Halton Gill, from the road that comes over from Malham Moor. Littondale is one of the loveliest dales in the National Park. It has stunning landscape, beautiful villages, and the people who live here all come together as one community.

When I look from the road top, down to the valley bottom and Halton Gill, I focus on the village rather than the landscape. The landscape is as big a part of planning as the buildings, but on a day to day basis it's the buildings that I work with. I've had involvement with half of the buildings in Halton Gill. There's Manor Farm, a lovely 17th century listed building, which sits prominently in the centre of the village. One of the local farmers has converted a barn nearby to a farm workers' house. This has worked out so well for them and for the village and I feel I really helped them to achieve this. That's a part of the job I love – building relationships and helping people through the process. I've felt really involved in the village community through my work – a lot of the residents know me, and driving through people wave or stop and talk. It's somewhere that's always nice to go back to.

Good development is something that respects the context, that doesn't harm the character and appearance of a place. It should ideally have a positive impact on the character and appearance, but sometimes the best thing you can achieve has a neutral impact or resolves some existing problem. As a planner, I get the opportunity to influence the development of the area. Most people will approach me early on and say 'this is what we want to do' and I'll help them to make it acceptable. One of the biggest issues is visual impact, and impact on the character of the area. Whilst we always aim for really high quality development, there is only so far we can go – we need to be realistic about what people can afford and what works for a farm or a house, but you can usually get positive results.

The downside of covering the southern dales is that I no longer visit the area when I'm not working. Before working for the Authority I would regularly go walking in Littondale and Wharfedale, but now I see planning issues everywhere and people recognise you as a planner. I don't think of the north of the Park – where I live – as work. I try not to get involved in any planning issues there; it's my home.

Tony Bullough

Ranger, National Trust

I've lived up here at Malham Tarn for 17 years. We get some cracking stars. When you're up here at night, you've no street lamps, there's nothing on horizon, and you've all these stars there in your face, so you take notice of them more.

Where this picture's taken from – it's just one of those places. When you're up there, on a nice day, you can see forever. You can see wind turbines going towards Bradford; you can see wind turbines behind Burnley; you can see right the way down to the west coast. If you turn around and look sort of north east-ish you're looking back up into the Dales: you can see Great Whernside; and if you turn round and look over the hill that's behind you, you're looking down Ribblesdale. It's just a great place to go and have a look.

If we're going up here, we'll be checking springs and water supplies. They aren't actually at the top of the hill, but you'll walk that extra five minutes up on to top, and have a right nice good look round. The springs are our main water supply, so we have to go up two or three times a year to make sure they're all right, make sure they're not blocked up – because if there's no water, you've nothing, have you?

We do grazing monitoring up here, to make sure it's not being overgrazed. We check on things like heather, and bilberries, and cranberries, and other moorland plants, to see how they're going. Because they're nice and tender, sheep will eat a lot of them. It works the other way; if you don't have enough stock up there, all this grass grows up and smothers them out. You've got to have that happy medium – in between.

There's a National Nature Reserve here, it's got every designation going for it. It's got internationally important wetland status – usually you get it for birds, but we got ours for plants and insects. There's an insect occurs on there somewhere that doesn't occur anywhere else in Great Britain – a wingless caddis.

I was born and brought up on a farm, but it wasn't big enough to support more than one family. So I went farming for a dairy farmer for two years. Then I went into the building trade for a bit. Then I got married and worked on a private estate for about five or six years. I've been working here just over 24 years. I like the variation. There's hardly ever two days the same. When you're farming you hardly met anybody, because you were working with animals all day; private estate you worked by yourself or with whoever was there helping you. When I came here, I started working with all sorts of different people: volunteers, other workmates, people from other properties.

We do all sorts of work with schools. It gets kids out doing something different from what they would do ordinarily. You get some kids out of town, and they're frightened to death of getting mucky. Taking them out and seeing something different is just brilliant.

Andrew Walter

Reserves Officer, Cumbria Wildlife Trust

Smardale Gill National Nature Reserve is owned and managed by Cumbria Wildlife Trust. Because of the old railway line there is a really level surface which you can push a wheelchair or buggy down. So there is access into the middle of nowhere, surrounded by wildlife and history, for just about anyone to get to.

Smardale is a fantastic place, but what this view does is set it in the landscape, which is remote. You've got the Howgills as a backdrop, then grazed farmed fields, then the nature reserve on the steepest slopes and Scandal Beck at the bottom. Scandal Beck's a fantastic river: it's home to white-clawed crayfish, a globally endangered species, and other river fauna like otter, kingfishers and dippers, salmon and trout, as well as flora like water crowfoot and butterbur.

This view has had a significant industrial past. The viaduct was designed and built by Sir Thomas Bauch to take coke from Durham to Barrow-in-Furness – where it was used in iron smelting – and then to take iron ore back. It's a really elegant viaduct; I don't think it ruins the landscape at all, I think it's an asset. You can also see lime kilns attached to the limestone quarry: they were used to turn the limestone into quicklime, which was then used in the steel industry.

The best part of it is not shown by the picture, and that is the wildlife. With the Wildlife Trust's management we're maintaining the wildlife, which is phenomenal – it's hard to walk on some areas of this reserve, just because there are so many orchids. The wild flowers are so abundant that they often outdo the grass.

I've been at the Trust since July 1994. I look after about eight reserves in total, including Smardale. My job's land management: it includes all aspects, from going out and rebuilding a bit of wall, or chopping down some scrub, or coppicing in the woods (with volunteers quite often), or writing management plans and agreeing them with Natural England, or seeking funding to do work.

I've got two incredibly keen volunteers – Nigel and Lois Harbron – who are there two days a week pretty much – they manage the site, not me! I just give them ideas of what to do and they do it.

Being here for this long is rewarding in terms of land management, because it's all very long term. You get a more interesting overview having stuck with it.

Habitats are my main concern, because if you get the habitat right then everything else should follow. Here you've got ancient woodland, limestone grassland, hay-meadowy type grassland, and bracken and scrub. These broad habitat types support many plants that may have been lost from the surrounding land. The diversity of the habitats and their structure then supports a host of animals from mammals to invertebrates. One of the interesting species you get at Smardale is the scotch argus butterfly, which is a very dark, almost black, butterfly with red wing markings and eye spots. There are only two populations in England: it's right at the southern end of its natural range, but it does very well on the reserve, so much so, they come up in clouds around your feet in early September.

The top wall lying where the bracken finishes was quite dilapidated when I took the reserve on; that was virtually rebuilt by a local waller called Cecil Capstick. Most of the other boundaries have also been fixed up. The area just beyond the viaduct we periodically clear of scrub, and that's one of the best places for bloody cranesbill and rock rose, that's where you see scotch argus, northern brown argus and it's also a good area for dark green fritillary. The most obvious improvement is that we've upgraded the footpath to be more accessible; that has to be a major achievement for the reserve.

Mostly though, I hope that the view hasn't really changed, because it was a special place when I first got to it. It didn't need restoring, just managing, maintaining, and maybe a little tweaking.

Margaret Taylor

Farmer, High Laning Farm (and founder of Dent Heritage Centre with husband Jim)

This is the area that's closest to my heart. It's glorious, it's magnificent, and it's natural. It makes me think about all the work that's been done here for generations, and how people used to live.

I grew up in Dent. My dad was a cow man, and my grandparents were farming up at Rivlin Cowgill. I came to High Laning as daughter-in-law. In the early days we had a little farm and a butcher's shop. Unfortunately, my first husband died – I don't think I'll have anything as sad happen to me again. We couldn't carry on with the butcher's shop, but that was maybe a blessing in disguise, because it was the start of interference from supermarkets and price cutting. We used to bottle our milk here, and it came eventually with the milk. You'd go with the milk some mornings and you knew very well that people had been buying from the supermarket. That was quite a heart-string puller, as a local person who was used to making a living.

Then I took a U-turn and decided it might be a good idea to try and go with tourists and set up a camping and caravan park. It was very difficult. It costs an absolute fortune to change from what you have been doing to something else, and then to have the heartache of people not being very happy about the changes. This was in 1970. Eventually we made it.

Our youngest son is still farming our farm – a very small area at High Laning Farm, High Ground, and what was my grandma's farm at Rivlin. He's happy – he loves his sheep. You're bred to it, aren't you? You either have it or you haven't it. I have it myself. I have the instinct of everything that goes on on the land, and so has this son of mine who's carrying on. His instincts are good. I'm all the time having a look. It's in my blood. I can't leave it alone. Being a widow, I did a lot of farming myself. Maybe because farming helped me carry on, it's closer to my heart. I would hate to think I couldn't walk out there and have a look at a few sheep and lambs, and feed the sheepdogs. When you're farming here you're very family-orientated. And farmers all help each other – they are really, really close.

Setting up the Heritage Centre has been a massive project. It tells the Dent story, if you like. I started off just collecting Dent postcards. My husband's brother was a collector too and we took quite a lot of his collection over. We were all over this area – if we heard there was something from Dent or the ten mile radius, we were there. Then my aunt died, and her legacy was enough to secure the building that's now the Heritage Centre. It was a 30 year project. We had such a great team working on it and we managed to get it open in 2006. I didn't know if I wanted to do it because Dent is very close to my heart, or if it's about sustainability – to make sure Dent keeps alive – I'm not sure.

We developed Flintergill Outrake Nature Trail too. That's quite something. As you walk up there it's something really out of this world because it's very unspoilt. There's a lot of fauna in there – the birds sing and it's very, very peaceful, very natural. Further up you get to the house where people used to live, at High Ground. I think about what a drudge it would have been up there – but they'd have been happy. Natural England helped us renovate the barn, so there's another little museum with all the implements they used to use on the farm. There's a lime kiln as well, and the quarry. Then if you walk a little further up you come to the Topograph, which shows the distance to all the hills: starting at Barbondale, down to the Howgills, Helmside Knot, Rise Hill, Knoutberry, then you come back round this side: Whernside, Deepdale, Great Comb.

You can do the trail and look at it the way it is today, or you could turn the clock back and think about how it was: think about the weavers' cottages at the bottom, where they used to weft the linen on the dancing flags, and how they used to tell the children the tales about the fairies.

Fran Graham

Wildlife Conservation Officer, Yorkshire Dales National Park Authority

This is a view of Juniper Gill in Moughton, which is part of the Ingleborough National Nature Reserve. Coming over from Horton-in-Ribblesdale you see just a scattering of old trees here on the plateau. Once you go down into that gill there are hundreds and hundreds of trees – it's quite otherworldly.

I'm a Wildlife Conservation Officer, and every year part of my work is to go out between mid-September and mid-October and collect juniper seeds from this site and the two others in the Park. Juniper is seen to be at risk in the UK, and because we have quite a lot of juniper in the Park it's one of our priorities to help to conserve it. It's also a conifer and there are only three native conifers in the UK – juniper, box and yew. Usually we wouldn't intervene in this kind of way, but with factors such as an ageing population, rabbits, deer, pests and disease, we think it's important to collect seeds and get them propogated properly. As climate change happens that's probably going to be another factor having an adverse effect on it. If we can try and bolster the populations, they've got more of a chance of adapting to that situation.

Juniper is very slow growing, so you often get these very wizened-looking trees. It takes them two years to produce seed. So at any one time, when you go seed collecting, you've got the very immature green berries that are not ready yet; the dark purple ones which are the ones you want; and then you've got the wrinkled up brown ones which are last year's, and they're all mixed together. They've also got very spiky leaves, so you get in a bath at the end of the day and you feel like a colander. We send the seeds to a specialist nursery who propogate them and when they're large enough the plants are available for planting within the National Park or other restoration schemes.

Juniper has separate male and female trees. The male flowers produce the pollen. The female flowers are actually tiny cones that open up and receive the pollen. Obviously the seeds are only present on the female trees. If you haven't got enough male trees present, and enough pollen produced, and enough wind-pollination happening, you're not going to get the berries. We call them berries but they are actually cones.

They are quite incredible-looking trees. Apparently people used to cut them down and use the wood to fuel illicit stills for whisky or whatever. The wood doesn't produce much smoke so they could do it on the quiet. It probably smells really nice as well. And of course juniper berries are one of the flavourings of gin.

Another thing to mention is that there are some birds which are specialist eaters of juniper berries, such as the ring ouzel. There are quite a lot of invertebrates that are supported by juniper as well – lots of spiders and little creepy crawlies.

There are two other places like this in the Park, both in Swaledale: one on Grinton Moor and one at Thwaitestones. There are some good public rights of way that go through or very close to these juniper populations. To get to this one on Moughton you can go up from Austwick, up Crummackdale, over the top of Moughton and down to Horton-in-Ribblesdale. That would go through the juniper population if the public want to see it. The one near Grinton has a very minor road going through it; you can see it from the roadside. The one at Thwaitestones, which is owned by the Woodland Trust – that's not quite so accessible, but you can see it really well just from the village of Thwaite. There are quite a lot of smaller populations up in the Swaledale area particularly; they tend to be about 50-100 trees at a time.

Juniper is just one of a number of rare species that I'm involved in working on. There are a lot of other wild flowers, mosses, lichens and fungi species, and each one's got its own interest. It's the best job in the world. It's getting out and about to beautiful places, and it's trying to protect it for a future generation.

Gail Smith

Community Worker, People and the DALES – Diversity, Access, Learning, Environment, Sustainability, Yorkshire Dales Millennium Trust

I work on an outreach programme called People and the DALES. We work with disadvantaged groups from the urban areas bordering the south of the Dales, bringing them up to the countryside. For many people it's the first time they've been out of the city and up to the Dales, so it's quite a special experience for them.

Oxenber Wood is just one spot we take people to. It's a fantastic area, particularly in spring because of the bluebells, orchids and other wild flowers. It's also relatively easy to get up high without too much effort for groups that aren't used to walking. They get that magical experience of being on high and looking down.

Most of our work is with groups from Bradford, Leeds and Keighley, but we work in north east Lancashire as well. We've built up good links with community groups, mental health groups, urban youth groups, people with disabilities, and many more. And then a big part of the work is with people from black and minority ethnic groups. It's about reaching those groups that haven't had the opportunity to be out before. We tailor-make the visits to each group, because they're so different in what they want and need.

We did a lot of evaluation this summer and found that the impact of the People and the DALES project on people's wellbeing and mental health has been really powerful. The other day a group leader described seeing the impact of the serenity in the countryside on people during these visits. He works with people with mental health problems and told me that during a visit one of his service users said: 'this is the first time I've ever felt like I don't need my medication'. You might think it's a fairly simple, standard thing, coming out for the day. But it isn't just a day out, it's about giving people that quiet space and quiet time to just be in the natural world and enjoy it. I think that's really powerful and really important, particularly for people from urban areas who often lead very busy, full-on lives a lot of the time.

We work a lot with refugees and asylum seekers. They have a tough life and are dealing with some very difficult situations. One of the really important things that's come from working with these groups is that it's given people a real sense of belonging. For a lot of them, seeing the English countryside for the first time, they're able to relate it to wherever they've come from. We have people standing there saying, 'wow this is just like Bangledesh', 'it's just like Pakistan', 'this is just like home'. People are able to open up and talk because it connects with things from their past. To be able to give people a chance to come and do something nice, something positive, to feel that 'yes, this is ours', 'we can come and enjoy this', is really important.

We're also seeing that people we've worked with are coming back, on their own, and with their families. Over the course of the project we have trained 57 community group leaders to give them the skills and confidence to be able to bring groups that they work with out for themselves. That's really working, which is fantastic.

The other way we try and link people more into the natural world is by doing conservation work with groups. We'll perhaps do a series of visits to begin with, so that they get familiarised and feel comfortable in the outdoors, then we'll encourage them to move on to other things. So we do drystone walling, woodland management, we take them out to hill farms and get them working with local farmers, park rangers and other local providers. So people are getting some practical skills and practical experience and that takes it a step further for them.

I just love giving people the opportunity to experience the natural world, and really be part of that. It's about enabling people to experience and share that sense of awe and wonder. Seeing the looks on people's faces when they do experience it is just magical; it's a pleasure.

Ceri Katz

Peatland Restoration Officer, Yorkshire Wildlife Trust

This is Booze Moor in Arkengarthdale. We're doing peat restoration work all around that area. I really enjoy working in this part of the Dales – at the most northern tip. It feels very different from the southern areas: a bit more remote, a bit more rough and ready.

Arkengarthdale has also been quite interesting because of all the different management that's taking place on the site. There's the grouse moor, and the farming, and it includes the historical management with the lead mines which are dotted around all over the place. It's been quite difficult to make sure we're not having any damaging impact on the historical environment, as well as trying to improve the landscape for its management today; Arkengarthdale encompasses all of that.

In spring it's fantastic, all the birds start to come out, so you've got lapwings and curlews, geese and oystercatchers. It's like everything comes back to life. There are times going through the winter when the only thing you can hear up there is the wind blowing, or the rain dripping off your clothing!

I suppose to take a photograph you're just taking that one pinpoint in time, but when you're actually out there you're taking in not only that area but the whole area around you, and also the sounds, and what you can feel as well – if it's a nice sunny day, or if there's a cool breeze – it's difficult to get that all in.

I've got an agricultural background. My parents own a farm in mid-Wales. They've got a relatively large area of peat and upland heath there, and there have been areas where they've tried to stop peat erosion. I've always been interested in that environment. I quite enjoy wandering around in it, even when it's windy and rainy – it's great.

It can take a while to see the impact of the restoration work we do. We've done work on some sites down in the southern area of the Dales, which were the first sites we worked on. It's been good to be able to see the difference it's made. You've got sphagnum colonising the pools behind the peat dams; and whole areas where it was just bare peat and nothing else growing, where now we're getting vegetation and heather coming back and cotton grass colonising the edges; that's been really satisfying.

Anthony Roberts

Landowner

My great-grandfather bought the Kilnsey Estate. He sadly never lived long enough to move here. My grandfather also died young, and so my father inherited it aged about eight. So it's been in the family since the beginning of the 20th Century. It was about 5-6,000 acres. Now I farm about 1,000 acres.

We started the trout farm here in 1978. It was just a tiny little raceway right at the top of the site. A raceway is where you farm your trout, it's essentially a pen where the water comes in one end and goes out the other. There was nothing else here on the site, except the old generating house. We discovered the quality of the water was ideal for producing trout, so we started selling to the public. The old generating house became our farm shop. We used to sell half a dozen trout in a plastic bag – they weren't even gutted in those days. And then we grew slowly, and we eventually built this farm shop and restaurant, selling locally-sourced foods. Now we produce about 35 tonnes of rainbow trout a year.

This particular area was just a field when we started. I tell the story about when I was still farming and I got an agricultural drainage grant because it was always a very boggy field. We tried to get the field better drained, but it didn't work. Our next idea was to excavate these two lakes out and open it up as a fishery. So we did all that – it was a huge job – and it worked very well really. Of all the water which comes through the trout farm, the majority of it feeds into the lake.

It's become a very popular spot for people to stop and take photos of the crag. It is part of the Turner Trail – Turner used to do a lot of painting in this area. He was commissioned to do a picture of the crag. No-one's ever discovered whether he actually completed it, but he did sketches of it – that's the only evidence they've got.

The crag was formed during the Ice Age. It's very unusual because it has this overhang at the top. Of course it's a Mecca for climbers. Some of these are 'free climbers' who use no ropes or pitons at all. Apparently they have to complete it in less than 20 minutes, because after 20 minutes your grip goes. My father once had a sheepdog that fell from the top to the bottom, and we thought, 'well that's it', but it got to the bottom, shook itself and ran off!

Just out of sight on the right is the show field that goes right down to Conistone Bridge. We have our annual show there in late August or early September. It gets an attendance of about 14,000 people a year. I suppose the three main features are a drystone walling competition, trotting races on the show field in the evening, and the crag race. They race up the side of the crag, back along the top, and they come down the chimney, through the trees and then out at the bottom there – that's one of the most hazardous and arduous fell races there is.

I've lived here all my life, and I just love the landscape. I think the older you get the more you appreciate it. I mean you go up on the hills where some of the views you get are fantastic, and you wouldn't get them anywhere else in the world. We have a lot of very nice people living up here; the communities are great, and the old farmers are tremendous characters.

I suppose everyone likes to think you leave a little bit of a legacy – like the lakes we've made – but when you're standing up there on the hills it makes you realise how transitory we are as human beings, when you compare how long all this has been here in the past, and how long it's hopefully going to be here in the future. I think part of your brief is to look after it and hand it onto the next person who will responsibly do the same thing.

Geoff Garrett

Senior Trees and Woodlands Officer, Yorkshire Dales National Park Authority

If anyone says 'show me the Dales' – this is the place to go. It's a view from Conistone Pie, which is quite a landmark as you go up the dale. The best way to get there is to walk up the valley from Conistone. Because you're walking up the valley, the view's not apparent to you until you get to the top. If you get the right day, it is an enormous view. Here, you're looking into the heart of the Dales, north towards Kettlewell.

I chose it because it's got Wharfedale on one side, and Littondale on the other side. They're both different types of dales, but both very special in terms of woodlands. They also reflect some of the work the Trees and Woodlands Team is trying to do to create woodlands and to protect our important existing woodlands.

On the Wharfedale side, you can see how these woodlands run with the contour. You've got a river in the bottom, you've got enclosed land, followed by woodland, followed by upper allotments, followed by moorlands. That is repeated in a very distinctive fashion all up Wharfedale.

Littondale is quite an open dale. It's not that well covered by trees on the south side, but we've done an awful lot of planting on the other side to connect up a lot of the ancient, semi-natural woodlands that are there; they're the jewels in the woodland crown.

Compared to the national average, the tree coverage here is very low. If you take the conifer plantations out, it's only about 2%. Conifer isn't natural here. Really we're famous for hanging ash woodlands. The way the limestone comes to the surface creates a very alkaline soil, which ash love.

This whole area, apart from maybe some of the very tops, would have been covered in woodland – we're talking a long, long time ago. People came here wanting to do farming, then we had the iron smelting, the lime production. That all required wood of some description, whether that's charcoal, or white coal, or just ordinary wood to burn and build with   so they took wood away. The

important ancient semi-natural woods that we have now are the woods that humans have left.

The average size of a woodland in the National Park is two hectares, which is tiny really. A two hectare woodland is quite vulnerable. If you were to create another woodland next to it, another one next to that, and connect that to another existing woodland, then that creates a whole woodland, which could be ten hectares in size, which gives it a much more robust feeling. It can deal with pressures on its habitat, on the environment. The pressures have been grazing in the past, but climate change now is turning into quite an issue.

I think it's agreed that climate change is happening, the question is what do we do about it? What do we, as advisers to people who own these woodlands, suggest happens? All you can do is say it's almost certain there's going to be a change, and we need to provide woodlands which are more robust. It's really about trying to create a framework for whatever happens, to help woodlands be more adaptable.

A thousand hectares of new native woodland has been planted over the last ten years or so – you've got to be proud of that sort of thing. The National Park Authority really didn't do it by themselves though – they had an awful lot of partners helping to fund it and do it.

I think with a lot of people there's a fundamentally good feeling about walking into a woodland, whether you're a city person, or wherever you come from. Maybe it makes you feel happier, or more able to cope with life, or more peaceful, but I do get a positive feeling when I walk into a woodland. Other people might get it when they stand on top of a moorland on a summer's day.

Allen Kirkbride

Farmer

I grew up on this farm. Going back when I was younger it was actually three different farms, it's now just one. I probably took it for granted that I'd farm – I didn't have a great desire to do a lot else and farming's sort of bred into you, I think.

Our land goes as far as the church, so all this land in the foreground is mine. This field at the front here is called the Giant's Cradle because of its shape. It's grazed by cows in the summer. The ones a bit further off are meadow land and are made into hay and silage. Come the spring they can be very colourful with quite a lot of wildflowers in them. I just like the area and how every field's different; there are no flat fields, they're all small hills.

What's dominant to Askrigg, wherever you take a picture from, is Addlebrough in the background. It's not very high, but it stands out and just makes the perfect view across.

We're forever drystone walling. There are bits dropping sort of continually. But these walls have been there 120/150 years, so they've done well. It's just a matter of keeping them there and keeping them tidy. The walls are great in lambing time, because a sheep with young lambs can get behind a wall if the weather's not at its best; they can get out of the wind and it keeps them dry.

That's Askrigg just on the left. You can't really see it from a lot of places – it's in a little valley and very well hidden. Going back, Askrigg is a little bit like Reeth; it's always been a working village. Years ago, while they used to have the lead mines on the moors, the lead miners would each have two or three fields; they'd keep a few animals and work in the mines at the same time. That's why round the village there are a lot of small fields.

I do quite a lot in the community. I'm chairman of the Parish Council and various other things. The voting population of the village is 450, so it's only small, but it's quite an industrious village – there's always something going on.

My grandparents rented the farm originally. They were cattle dealers. My father did a bit of that, but we went more into the farming and the milk. We milk the cows, but we also bottle all our own milk; we pasteurise and separate it and we retail in Wensleydale and upper Swaledale. We deliver milk to the shops in Reeth and Muker, and some B&Bs in between; then we'll go down as far as West Burton, and up to Hawes. So we go through some really scenic little villages on our round. Going back a lot of years, every farmer would milk their cows and sell the milk around the village – it's quite a rarity now.

What I like about this type of farming particularly is that the seasons are all so different, and the views are different. Every day with the way the weather and the seasons are – it's changing all the time. And no matter where you go in the upper dales you have a marvellous view. If you like scenery then there's no better place to be than in the Dales.

Gary Verity

Chief Executive, Welcome to Yorkshire and Sheep Farmer

For me, this is me coming home, along the road out of Middleham up to the Gallops. When you look around you get a contrast of different scenery straight away. You've got Pinker's Pond down to one side of you; you've got these big hills in the distance; you've got Braithwaite Hall there. You're entering Coverdale. You're entering the National Park, which of course is a special place to many of us.

This picture gives the impression it's quite flat, but you are entering a proper glacial valley. Each of the dales has their own distinctive shape, determined by the kind of glacier that was in there: so Swaledale with that narrow V-shape; Wensleydale with that huge U-shape. Coverdale's something in between. It's less well known than the other dales, and is less commercialised if you will, but it's just as beautiful as any of the dales. It was known as the artists' dale because of the light; Turner painted in Coverdale a lot.

We're looking towards the farm that has been my home for 20 years now. I've spent more years living here than anywhere else in my life. Although some people say it's very remote, it's not actually remote. Everything's relative; this is just a few more minutes away from metropolises.

We used to have quite a big flock of sheep, relatively speaking. My wife died three years ago so I now rent quite a bit of the land out, but I still have enough sheep to keep me busy. I didn't grow up on a farm, but I always had a love of animals, which the James Herriot books helped cement. I think there are probably two things you would want to do as a Yorkshire man if you could: one is to play cricket for the county, the other is to have sheep in Yorkshire. I've been lucky enough to do one of those. Next year I start as President of the Scarborough cricket festival, but my cricket-playing days are probably not really going to happen now.

The sheep soon bring you back down to earth. They are not interested in what you've done in your corporate life; not interested in who you've had meetings with or how the meetings

have gone. They're completely classless, and they will stand on your foot regardless of how successful a week, day, month, year you think you've had. The farm is where I can maintain my sanity.

I think as a farmer you've always got that awareness of your fragility and your reliance upon the weather and the landscape and the elements, and the respect you need to have for them. So I've always had that – I hope.

I've been the Chief Executive at Welcome to Yorkshire since September 2008. I lead this team, and hopefully help corral and cajole and inspire them to do the great work that they do. We look to grow the Yorkshire economy, primarily through tourism, but not exclusively. I like the variation of the job. We meet so many great people from different businesses from all across Yorkshire. I get to travel around the great county of Yorkshire. We get to do wonderful projects like bringing the start of the Tour de France to Yorkshire.

It's not a difficult ask is it? If you ask a Yorkshire man does he want to be responsible for marketing Yorkshire, and salesman chief for Yorkshire? It's one of the greatest honours you could be offered.

We're very lucky in Yorkshire – we've three National Parks and they're all different and very distinctive. We have three Areas of Outstanding Natural Beauty too, and they're all distinctive. We have a stunning coastline. All of those things added together mean that we are very blessed. You can see why people call it God's own county.

There's atmosphere when you're in the Yorkshire Dales National Park. Whatever time of year, whatever time of day, there's always something very special there. I think it's very spiritual. There's an authenticity about it – you know you're in a very real place.

Miles Johnson

Countryside Archaeological Adviser, Yorkshire Dales National Park Authority

This is one of my favourite views, coming down off Booze Fell on a walk that I've done quite often. I like the mix; it's very scenic but there's a lot of industry in there. Booze is a fabulous name. It's alleged to have an old English origin, but I wonder if it might be a corruption of Boose or Bouse, which is a term that's used for lead ore.

Arkengarthdale is one of the most historically industrialised parts of the National Park. Most people don't think of it as an industrialised landscape at all, but it's as industrial as places like the Nottinghamshire coal fields, or some of the slate mining landscapes in Wales. There was large scale intense lead mining over much of the higher ground. The bit at the top of the photo is Fremington Edge. The pink colour is the colour of the waste materials from the ore processing. That big gulley is entirely manmade; it's called Fell End Hush. Hushing is a way of mining; a kind of open casting. Originally there might have been lines of mine shafts down there, but after a while going down in little shafts becomes impractical, and it's actually easier to open cast. They used torrents of water to wash away all of the top soil. If you had enough water you could actually use it to help move rock. Eventually, over hundreds of years, this huge scar through the landscape formed.

The really intensive mining was happening in the 18th and 19th centuries, but it was going on for a long time before that, probably back into the medieval period, possibly during the Roman period. In the 1880s the mines here were undercut by foreign imports of lead. Overnight the industry almost stopped, and the population effectively halved in places like Swaledale and Arkengarthdale, which is why buildings like the one you can see here became redundant.

People have different views of dereliction in the landscape. Being an archaeologist I quite like it, but to other people it could be really unsightly. To me it's fascinating – we've got hundreds of years of history, and an amazing amount of labour embodied in the landscape, but to other people it's just industrial waste.

It's a great shot, but it's not quite so revealing in terms of field patterns. They're very topographically determined, because you've got quite limited land that's any good. The villages tend to be located near the good ground. There's no arable farming here now, but there would have been tonnes of it in medieval times. You can still see terraces near some villages, which were cultivated for planting, and ridge and furrow patterns in some of the fields.

There's an awful lot of prehistory in the area. On top of Fremington Edge there are things called ring cairns, which are about 20 or 30 foot across. They're kind of slight, just a ring of stones. Somewhere in the middle of them, underground, there'll be a hole with a cremation urn. They're basically the predecessor of barrows (burial mounds). These would be from the Early Bronze Age.

I provide advice to farmers, land managers, land owners and organisations on how to look after archaeological features in the landscape: how to manage them well, or manage them better, and how to avoid damaging them. It involves making decisions about what you value about the past. We're interested in managing anything that's basically redundant and has some historic interest, from really obscure stuff – like ancient tree remains at the base of the peat that will go back 8,000 years – to things as recent as the Second World War. It's about finding ways to keep the past surviving wherever we can, and to do that in a way that accepts that people have to make a living, and manage a landscape. It's very much a balancing act.

Alison O'Neill

Farmer, Shacklabank Farm

It's timeless is that view; absolutely bleakly beautiful. It's the only place in the Howgill Fells where you really feel like the Ice Age made any impact, because it's the only place where you've got the U-shaped valley gouged out; everywhere else is rounded and soft. It just creates this absolute drama. And it's higher than it looks here, when you're up there you feel like you're on the top of the world.

It's so special because Rough Fell sheep graze here – that's the breed of sheep I keep. My grandfather would always say 'there are no flowers in the Howgill Fells, but the flowers of the fellside are the sheep'. They were originally bred for wool. They're larger sheep, long legged, with beautiful temperaments. Also my fell pony stallion came from Cautley Crag; he would have grazed on here.

At the bottom of Cautley Crag here there's a small Temperance Inn – The Cross Keys. My grandparents lived at the foot of the Howgills and, before they were married, Granddad invited Grandma for a walk across the Howgills. So Grandma would have stood here looking at the view and thought how beautiful it was. They walked down the valley bottom here, went into The Cross Keys, had ham and eggs and he asked her to marry him.

I was born in Sedbergh at the foot of the Howgills on a family farm. When I was 16 I left home and travelled. I didn't think I wanted anything to do with it because it was hard work. But when I was in my late 20s I suddenly wanted to return to the land, and so I came back.

I came here with £60 and nothing else; I was a month off having Scarlet, my daughter. It's a really hard living to make. I know some people think it's being a bit dramatic, but it is kind of tough. There have been a couple of times when I could have just given the farm up, thinking 'this is crazy'. But it's the life I've always wanted. It's kind of like you're born to it. I love the land, and animals, and I wanted to give Scarlet the life I had – to give her that freedom, and those choices, and to grow up in a beautiful place that's very safe.

We thought we were doing OK, and then Foot and Mouth came and wiped everything clean, and we had no money. It was horrendous. I kind of felt that a lot of it was my fault – because I'd wanted the farm and a lot of people had said financially it wasn't a good idea.

So then I thought – 'what else can I do?' I like walking and I like people, so I trained to be a walking guide. The idea was just to do a few walks from the farm – to sell the view. I won a competition with Country Living Magazine with this whole concept of a farm holiday and got some PR through that. Six months after that people came here from The Independent, The Daily Telegraph, lots of glossy magazines, and then the holidays started to sell. It went really well. Then I started getting calls from ladies who wanted to buy the clothes I was wearing in the pictures – which seemed crazy – so then I decided to make up some skirts and waistcoats using tweed. I now have a factory make them for me.

I still do the walks, and I do the tweed, and I go and give talks. I still farm – my sister and other members of the family come and help out. I have 250 of my own sheep, but I shepherd others. We call it stick and dog gathering – that's what I do. I don't have a quad bike; I have a fell pony and try and do it in the old fashioned way, just walking the hill looking at the sheep. Most people don't have time for that, but it's kind of how I was brought up.

I do talks for all kinds of groups – farmers' groups, landowners, WI – and I have so many letters from people that say I've inspired them to go back to the land: to start working on the land again, to get businesses going. People think you need money but then realise it's more about passion.

My granddad always said that what was important was having that land beneath your feet, and having a view, and knowing it was yours. Of course we never really truly own anything; it's all kind of everybody's. I really do live off the view though. If I didn't have a view I wouldn't have a business.

Roger Gibson

Drystone Waller, Fencer and Landscape Contractor

This is Lower Littondale. It's just above the village of Hawkswick, on Hawkswick Moor, looking back down towards Cracoe Fell and the bottom end of Wharfedale. I chose it because a lot of my work's based round here, and it is a cracking view. Wherever you look there, we've worked: we've drystone walled, we've planted trees.

We make up all the walls in that area. So if a gap falls, we go to it. There's a drystone wall, just down here near the river, that we restored. It was a 120 metre stretch that needed completely rebuilding. It's part of an ongoing restoration programme that the local farmer's doing. I've said many times that the drystone walls are like a jewel in the National Park's crown – they've got to be maintained.

These walls, because they're dry, they do move. You've got your dry weather and your wet weather and your frost and your snow, and unless they're maintained, eventually they become very loose. It gets to a point when it's easier to pull it all out and rebuild it from scratch – that's what we did with this wall here. It took us about 22 days.

When you pull an old existing wall, you've got all the materials there, because it's been built before. It's a little bit like a jigsaw, you've got to have an eye for it. When you rebuild it you rebuild it in your own style, so you may put some stones in differently than the chaps before you. We often remark on how the old guys would have done it, as we're building these walls.

These walls are dug out and then built with an A frame. You start with your big stones at the bottom – your footings – and then you slowly build up and finish with your small stones at the top. You need two or three rows of what we call throughs, which are stones that go right through and connect each side. And then, in all of it, you've got your filling – you pack the wall to make it strong.

I come from a farming background. It's not just working with livestock on a Dales farm, a lot of it is building walls and hedging and fencing; that's the part that I've taken on into my landscaping work.

I was taught to wall by someone, but I was often sent off on my own. I think the first wall I put up fell down, twice. And the third time I remember thinking, 'I'm not going to go back again, this is it now' – that was a good learning curve.

I love my work. It's satisfying to create out of natural things. I look upon it as an extension of a lot of the skills that I learnt on the farm in Sedbergh.

There's no place like the Yorkshire Dales anywhere in the world. When you go travelling anywhere, the best thing about it is coming back – a lot of local people tell you that. You can never beat that feeling you get when you come past Kilnsey Crag and turn into Littondale, it's a special place.

Dave Tayler

Deputy Director, Yorkshire Dales Millennium Trust

My connection with the Dales, and Ribblesdale in particular, goes back many years. Growing up as a southern lad, we used to come on family holidays to the Dales. In later years I studied geology and geography and grew to understand the landscape and the factors that shape it. I was attracted north to Sheffield University, which was the first time I lived in Yorkshire.

In the first week at Sheffield I went on a trip with the Caving Society, which on reflection was a fairly terrifying experience. We stayed in the caving club building in Horton-in-Ribblesdale; so that was my first real taste of the Dales, crawling around underground! A year later I came as a budding geologist to Horton, training to map the local rocks. Those were great experiences with friends; out exploring the landscape, learning how to measure, understand and read it – combined with work for the pub landlord, helping on his farm stacking straw for the winter and having a lot of fun. That week left a real impression on me, an incredibly positive one.

Over the following years there were coincidences that brought me back here: wandering across Malham Moor and visiting Tarn House; hitch hiking from the Lake District through Settle and over Buckhaw Brow, before the by-pass was built, and seeing the view of Giggleswick Scar and Settle. All these memories were steadily building up a connection with the place.

Life then took me all over the world in environmental education and adventuring: to South Devon, Asia, the Antipodes and then to South Africa. In 1997, I landed a post with the Field Studies Council at Malham Tarn Field Centre. I've lived in Ribblesdale ever since, only a few miles south from that experience I had as a young geology student. I spent five years working at Malham Tarn and I must have travelled up and down the hill to Langcliffe Brow en route to Malham with thousands of students, colleagues and friends. I would often stop and get them to sit on the limestone and take in this view. For me it's the richness of the dale in terms of the human activity that's shaped how it looks. It's not a pristine one by any stretch of the imagination, but for a geographer that's all part of the rich tapestry that makes up a view.

In the backdrop there are the Three Peaks and in particular the massif of Ingleborough. There is the quarried landscape at Helwith Bridge with the striking exposures of gritstone and limestone. The caravan site in Little Stainforth marks the importance of visitors to the area's economy. The River Ribble, the wonderful limestone terraces, meadows and field patterns, field barns and walls, the winding Settle-Carlisle railway, the pockets of woodland and the glaciated faults at Stainforth Scar. This view is constantly changing throughout the year and is something I have got strongly attached to.

I have worked at the Yorkshire Dales Millennium Trust for 11 years which has enabled me to widen my involvement in the Dales. We have developed a very successful outreach, training and education programme which has supported a broad range of people to come and enjoy and understand the landscape. My work also involves developing practical conservation work. It is a true privilege to be in a place I love, able to shape and support how it might evolve in decades to come with a group of wonderful, dedicated, passionate, inspiring people.

I was lucky enough to have those formative experiences as a young person – I had great teachers and people who really inspired and excited me to find out why the landscape looks like it does. Those are magic moments in life – the sparks – which have led to a lifetime of fulfilment and enjoyment. Now I'm in a position where I think, 'great, I can create those sparks for other people'. They don't all catch fire, but some of them will.

David Butterworth

Chief Executive, Yorkshire Dales National Park Authority

No matter how good a photographer is, they can't really capture the essence of 'place'. You really need to be there to appreciate it. It's a whole landscape experience.

I picked this view because it's unusual in Dales' landscape terms. It represents a different kind of landscape, in the north of the Park. I also picked it because of its political significance. The current boundary of the Park goes right along the top of the Howgills. So you can stand at the highest point – on the Calf – with one foot in and one foot out of the Park, thinking, what's this all about? It represents for me man's stupidity about designating landscapes on political, administrative, or bureaucratic boundaries, rather than for the value of the landscape itself.

That particular boundary was designated in 1954; it's the boundary between Westmoreland and the West Riding, as was. And here we are in 2013, and we're just about, hopefully, to sort out that unfinished business and designate the whole of the Howgills. For me, that would be a fantastic professional achievement. Natural England have been carrying out a review of the boundaries of the Yorkshire Dales and the Lake District for about two and a half years, or for 54 years, depending on how far you take it back! We expect a decision by the end of 2013. It's a big deal. It would make the Park about 25% bigger – a substantial increase in landscape.

I walk in that area quite a bit. The Park is 680 square miles, but finding solitude and feeling that sense of isolation and the spiritual feeling you get with that, is very difficult. You get it in the Howgills in a way you don't get it in other areas. If you're in that particular landscape for any length of time it is like a spiritual experience. The most amazing thing is the contrast between this sense of isolation and the fact that the M6 and the West Coast Mainline is half a mile away from you. You get these massive infrastructure projects cutting right through the middle of that landscape. You get all that traffic noise and the noise of the railway

and then you turn a corner and you can't hear a thing. To be in a National Park and see these huge projects is quite bizarre, but I love it. I think buildings or structures like railway viaducts can have a hugely positive impact in many cases. Whenever they're first put there there's an absolute hue and cry, but they become such a significant part of any landscape. What it shows for me is the interaction between man and the landscape, which is just brilliant, assuming we don't bugger it up and build inappropriate structures!

I've worked in the Park since 1991, and been Chief Executive since 2001. I'm not a planner or an -ologist, I'm not from that kind of background. My skills, for what they are, and my experience as a Chief Executive, are in terms of driving performance through the organisation. So the things I'm most proud of are the collective things: the fact that the performance of this National Park Authority is as high as any in the UK. Every year we sweep a load of awards for what we do both inside and outside of the Authority; for work on the Limestone Country Project, for major construction projects, for low carbon emissions. When I see the performance across the organisation, and see how that motivates people, particularly at this difficult time (because we've lost so many staff with the recent cut backs) that's what I'm really proud of.

Gary Lodge

Farmer, Westside Farm

I didn't know where to choose really, I just like it round here. This is above Langcliffe, looking back over where I work, land that we farm, our house, and Pen-y-Ghent in the background.

I like this view because all the walls are actually up, whereas on quite a bit of land they're not maintained that well. We try and keep them up – I think it's important, round here, to keep it how it was, and how it should be. I do quite a bit of walling. In the autumn, when we're not so busy at home, I go out and do drystone walling for other people. It's something I quite like. I learnt walling from my dad – I just went with him and picked it up, and then just practiced really. It's quite rewarding when you've done it and it looks tidy.

I've lived here since I was one. I always helped Dad when I was a kid, and I just enjoy it really. I like the variety – different stuff every day, and looking after stock. We have about 1400 sheep, about 6-700 acres of land, and we rent some as well. So a lot of what you can see here is land we work on. It's a nice area to work in, most of the time.

We used to have about a hundred cows of our own. Now we just take in other people's cows, for summer and for winter, at so much a head. We sold the cows a few years ago because I'm more interested in the sheep.

I do a lot of showing prize sheep each year. We take the best ones and compete against other farmers. It's a hobby really, and it's showcasing your sheep, so when you go to sell them they're worth more. It depends what breed you're on as to what's important: with Swaledale it's all about markings – the colourings on the face and the legs; with some other sheep, like Texels, it's about the shape and muscle they have; we have Swaledales mainly.

I like working with stock, and I enjoy lambing time. If you look after them properly, it's rewarding. You buy a tup and see how his offspring is. You keep trying to improve what flock you have. We enjoy showing, and trying to better ourselves all the time.

Dad always used to give us a sheep for our birthdays or for Christmas, and we would look out for that one when we were feeding. We still have favourites now – often the show ones; if they've done well in a show, you keep a look out for them. I don't remember getting upset as a kid when they were killed, I think if you're brought up with it you get used to it.

You do get to know the sheep and a lot of them we'll recognise because you see them every day. They all look the same to most people, but they're completely different, with different personalities. You have some that seem to always graze in a particular part of the field, or two or three of them who are always together. It's as if they have friends and stick to them – they're quite human like that.

Roy Lingard

Head Forester, Bolton Abbey and Chatsworth Estates

The reason I love this place is that you can go and stand by the waterfall and you can't see any of the modern landscape. You can go down there and imagine yourself back in a sort of a wild wood – it's all nice gnarled, old trees. It's just fantastic. The Valley of Desolation got its name after a storm in 1836. It devastated the area, hence the name; before that it was called Posforth Gill I think.

Apart from it being a beautiful place, I was asked to plant the area in 1996/1997. We wanted to try to restore some of the ancient woodlands that have been lost over many centuries, and the trees are also shelter for farm stock as well.

At that time everyone was harping on about the traditional Dales landscape, which is a complete myth. The landscape of stone barns, stone walls, open areas, a farmed hay meadow landscape, only started to evolve in about the 1750s. If you go back to 8 – 5,000BC it would all have been mostly wooded. I did quite a lot of research on how the landscape's evolved since the last Ice Age, and I thought it would be a good idea to plant the different phases of woodland development since the last Ice Age.

I wanted to make an educational walk. The area we've planted is along a very linear route: from Bolton Abbey village straight through the Valley of Desolation, you pass two waterfalls, and then go onto the moors. It's also interesting geologically. So as well as the individual tree evolution, we've done a trail that illustrates how the Ice Age shaped the landscape. We've planted different areas: starting off at the Arctic tundra phase; then through the Boreal phase and Atlantic phase; we've got an area showing the woodland as it might have been today if we hadn't chopped it all down; and an area with native-type woodland. It's a long term project and it's still evolving. My intention is to have the whole story from Arctic tundra through to modern forestry, and to explode this myth that the Dales landscape has always been as it is now and always should be.

I'm Head Forester for Bolton Abbey and Chatsworth Estates and keep an overview of both estates. We've got a commercial woodland here where we sell timber. We've also got areas of continuous cover, like Strid Wood, which are managed primarily for conservation. It's quite a varied and interesting job. I've been here 28/29 years now. I started off as a woodman, and then I got sent to college part time over a five year period. I took over from my predecessor here about 16 years ago.

We are starting to plant more woodlands in the UK, which is overdue, but we still need to plant a lot more. It's a resource from my point of view – over 80% of our timber needs are imported from abroad. We're too reliant on imports. We've got a really good tree growing climate here and we could do a lot more. I think it would be nice to get some of our woodlands back to where they used to be, for habitat reasons, conservation reasons, but also for economic requirements.

You've got to think in decades in forestry, even centuries. In Strid Wood we're planning what we want the woodland to be like in 200 years time. The beauty of working on a private estate is that we think on a long term landscape level. We all think of ourselves as stewards now for the next generation, and we're taking over from previous ones. We've got forest records going back to 1810, so you've got that continuity. You get the whole picture and you can put these long term things in place. It's not a job where you can go for three or four years and then move on; it's a way of life that you embrace or you don't.

Kevin Milburn

Farmer

This is taken from Spice Gill Allotment, where the sheep go in the summer. I like that view because when I'm up there feeding sheep, no matter how bad a day or nice a day it is, the viaducts are always stood there. I often think how much work and effort went into making them. I think everybody nowadays is in such a big rush; life goes by too fast. Sometimes I think you have to make time just to take it in.

I farm about 400 sheep and I've got 20 cows now. You try and better yourself every year, you try and get your stock better. It keeps us busy. We do a lot of drystone walling in the dale too, for farmers.

I've always walled. I just picked it up from my dad. It's the kind of thing you just have to learn for yourself to a certain degree – the more you do the better you get at it. It's not something you can really read out of a book. You have to keep going and doing bits, and then you get shouted at a few times when it's not right. It's a seasonal kind of thing – you don't want to be walling when it's right wintery and horrible. It's more a summertime job.

We can get some bad weather, that's why we try to keep all our inland walls up. A lot get left to go down, which is a shame. We try to keep ours up, and replant our hedges. A lot of folk just cut their hedges, but you cut them for so long and then they just die out in the bottom, and then lambs start walking through. With a good hedge, your stock shouldn't be able to get through. And with proper good hedges, little lambs go in and nibble out bits of leaves – that's nourishment for them as well.

You're in the heart of sheep farming up here. I grew up five miles down the road. My dad was a builder, but we've always had a few sheep. I always knew I wanted to work outside. I've been farming round here for about ten years now.

I like it in the autumn, because everything's looking at its best. This year's been a struggle getting fodder, but usually you've got all your fodder there, ready for winter. It's busy in autumn, because you're rudding the tups, and you want your different colours for your different weeks in lambing time. Every day we're going round all our tups marking the chests. So say if we louse on the 5th November the sheep will be due on the 1st April. We usually start with yellow; so all your yellow-bummed sheep are due the first week, and so on with the different colours. Then the sheep go up onto this high ground, and we feed them through to the middle of March. Usually January time we have them scanned, see how many lambs they're having. Come March you bring them down off the hills, and set them up into the different colours. Lambing time's busy: April into May. The ewes with one lamb go back onto the hills, and the ewes with two lambs stop down in the pastures – they need a bit better grass. Middle of May when the ewes come up onto the top fields, our meadows get cleared, ready for growing your crops – silo and hay. We usually harvest the end of June/July. Then all the sheep are clipped end of July. Then usually in August we take all the lambs off. They get sold about September/October time. And then you start all over again.

I'm probably at the point where I wouldn't want to get any bigger. I enjoy working for other farms – we do a lot of helping each other out: I'll go and clip for one of my mates, and then they'll come and help me clip – it works like that. If I got much bigger I wouldn't have time to go and help my other friends. And then it gets a bit lonely. You can have a long winter sometimes; when you're not dealing with folk all the time, they can be long days. So I like to work alongside folk.

Carl Lis

Chair of the Yorkshire Dales National Park Authority

It's a dramatic landscape here. When you're driving you can see Ingleborough from a long way away. In the summer, some of the views you get of it, with a bit of cloud or whatever, are just beautiful. I saw it every single day when I was working in the quarry. I used to go and have a walk on the lower slopes, to get away from the desk. Ingleborough to me is the most beautiful of the Three Peaks. It's iconic. You get different views from different areas, and it's a beautiful backdrop.

It's not just about Ingleborough, though, it's the setting of Ingleborough. I chose this view because of where I live, and the countryside that I live within, and because it reminds me of the community that I live within. The community is the lifeblood of the area. People are always open and welcoming. If you have a Yorkshire friend, you really have a terrific friend.

The quarry's not far away from this image. It's a gritstone quarry. The stone's quite rare. It's an intrusion into what's basically a limestone area. Its qualities are best described as a stone that wears quite slowly and presents a rough surface in the top matrix of a road's surface, that provides grip to a car's tyres. There are so few deposits in this country that exhibit these qualities.

I finished my working career as a quarry manager. I started out as an apprentice electrician, and then moved up through the ranks in quarrying. The job of quarry manager in Ingleton came up. I applied for it and got it, and moved up here. I retired five or six years ago now, but I still feel some affinity with the people who work within it. There's a good deal of skill in what they do, and they've worked a large slice of their life creating and nurturing that skill. It isn't just a question of going in with explosive and blasting it out and selling it; it's creating a product that can achieve the benefits in terms of road safety that I mentioned earlier.

When I worked at the quarry, I gradually started dealing with the National Park, and realised that it was an organisation that I really felt at home with. The world of quarrying was traditionally one of confrontation – constant confrontation between environmentalists and the quarrying companies. I think it's fair to say that the attitude's changed now. Certainly I felt that consultation was always better than confrontation.

I became a Member of the National Park Authority when I was a quarry manager, which was unusual to say the least. I've been the Chairman of the Yorkshire Dales National Park Authority, with a year's break, since 2004. I have to say that I have never worked for an organisation where as many people are so dedicated to what they do. Being Chairman has been simply the most enjoyable thing I've ever done in my life, by a considerable margin, because of the quality of the people that I have come into contact with. There are so many high points, far too many to single out one. Although when you see that school children from Horton-in-Ribblesdale have worked with schoolchildren from Keighley to build a wall on the top of Pen-y-Ghent, or we've created some more accessible footpath, it can make you feel so proud. That sense of achievement when you see people walking, enjoying the countryside and appreciating this unique landscape that we call the Yorkshire Dales - yes, that's simply great. That's what we are all about.

Amanda Owen

Shepherdess, Ravenseat Farm

This is the view from the top of our allotment looking back onto Ravenseat, and away and beyond. I think it's a really special view because it's timeless; there's no hint at all of the modern world. You can go up there and sit – as we often do when we're feeding the sheep – and you think to yourself you're doing the same job as our ancestors would have done. You feel a bit of a connection really, with times past.

If you go back to 1520 there were a lot of people living here – there was a lot more going on. People would go out and stay with the sheep and move them from place to place. That's why, dotted around our farm, we have 42 barns and little buildings.

All these fields and all these places have names. Everything's there for a reason, and that's what I like. I'm always telling the children all the names of the places because there's some wonderful names. As you go out onto the road end, you've got Ashgill, Knoutberry, Coldbergh Edge, you've got Whamp, you've got White Spots. If you get a map nowadays it just says how many hectares – it doesn't tell you the names; you lose the connection of where it is.

I like the fact that when you get a hill farm the hefted sheep come with it, because these sheep have lived here since time began, they know the place. On Birkdale Common, which we are looking across to, you have rights to run a certain number of sheep, but there are no boundaries. Other people's sheep also run up there, but yours stay in their place. Some do stray, but basically they know where they live; they're what they call 'hefted', each has a heaf mark. So we'll get the gimmer lambs – the females – in off Ravenseat and we'll put a red mark over the middle of the back, or the shoulder, or the loin, which tells us which part it lives on. It then goes back with its mother and it learns its patch; then it has its lamb and it teaches that.

So you see when Foot and Mouth came and a third of our flock were killed, everyone said 'well why don't you just buy some more sheep?' You can't, because how will they know where they live? It's inbred in them, a bit like a homing pigeon – they have their patch. We've just had to breed back up. It's taken until now to get back to where we were.

Me and my husband were both townies: I'm from Huddersfield, he's from Doncaster. Clive moved up here as a child and got the farming bug; he followed the local farmers about and knew he wanted to farm. Eventually he got himself a field and a few animals, it grew from there, and he ended up getting a tenancy on Ravenseat.

I watched too much All Creatures Great and Small on the television. I watched it and thought, 'ah, that is just wonderful – I want to be a shepherdess'. Can you imagine what happens when you tell your careers teacher that?! I got as much experience as I could – I went all over the place: lambing at one place, dipping at another, clipping, and basically learning as I went along. I did what I needed to do: walling, even working on a saw bench once, just whatever was required.

I was living in a caravan for a while, working on different farms, milking cows and shepherding. The fellow I was milking cows for asked me to pick up a tup for him. I came here, to Ravenseat, in the dark, and I thought 'oh my god where have I come to?!' And there was Clive, all on his own. We got the tup loaded into the trailer and then he rang me all week until I agreed to a date, and now here I am, all those years later. It does feel strange that in a roundabout kind of a way, from sitting as a child in Huddersfield and watching James Herriot on the television, I've come to here where the Herriot series was filmed. I feel that I have done a full circle.

Annie Hamilton-Gibney

Community Archaeology Project Development Officer

I think these views take over a little bit of your heart and soul. This is looking from an archaeological site – a roof slate quarry site on Mallerstang Edge – across the valley where I live, to Wild Boar Fell, one of the distinctive mountains that fascinates me.

This site isn't one of the ones that I've discovered in the valley, but I like it because it's enigmatic. I can't find any written evidence about it, so there are all these questions that haven't got answers. That's one of the things about being an archaeologist, you're always reading the landscape; it's like a big detective story where you're trying to put together the pieces. Sometimes you can find historical records that help with those pieces, but most of the time you're looking at sites that nobody knows about, and trying to work out what people were doing there.

When this site was recorded, many years ago, it was marked down as a slate quarry, but the geology isn't actually slate. I think they were quarrying roofing flags, which is where the confusion has arisen. In days gone by, when they didn't have vehicles, the quarry workers would have taken their horses and carts up there and worked away for the week, then come home, probably to Kirkby Stephen or down to Outhgill in Mallerstang at the weekends. When you go up there, there's a little village of workmen's huts, which would have been a home from home for them.

I'm a pre-historian, so my favourite sites, especially the ones I've found in the valley, are prehistoric; all you've got to go on is what you can read in the landscape. Over the years I've become an amateur geologist as well as a professional archaeologist. You need to be able to read what's geologically natural in the landscape and then be able to identify the manmade or the man-altered features, and then work out reasons for those alterations.

My most notable find in Mallerstang is a Neolithic enclosure, just to the right of this view. I'd found a lot of flint tools in the valley, which are evidence of prehistoric people living, working and trading here. I knew there were no recorded prehistoric monuments in the area, so I went looking in all the obvious places, and there it was, a 'causewayed-type' enclosure, sitting on the hilltop. It's not very distinctive, and it's not at all photogenic! It's one of those features that's been hiding in plain sight for nearly 6,000 years. These enclosures are signs of people from the first farming communities meeting together. In Mallerstang, we don't have a Parish Council, we have a parish meeting and I have the dubious privilege of being the Chair. To be Mallerstang's Chair and then to have found the first ever place where the parish 'meetings' started all those thousands of years ago, that was a really special moment. It's lovely to have put it on the record.

That exploration is part of human nature. People go to the moon, or the bottom of the sea, or wherever, without realising that there are sites on our own doorstep that are undiscovered that can be explored. I first set foot in this valley when I was ten years old. I've always loved living here, even before I studied archaeology. But having grown up and roamed around these fells for donkeys' years, it's surprised me that I couldn't see what I was looking at for so long. Studying archaeology is like having a veil lifted: suddenly you're looking at an entirely different landscape. Once your eyes have been opened you can't ever just go for a walk and enjoy the view, because you're always questioning what you're looking at, you're always trying to work out what people have done there before. You look at the landscape in a completely different light.

Tessa Levens

Peatland Restoration Officer, Yorkshire Wildlife Trust

This view's from Stags Fell, which is above Simonstone near Hawes, in Wensleydale. It's one of our peat restoration sites. I did the peat survey behind where this is taken.

It's very rare that we get to see a view like that: we're normally in hill fog or drizzle or something, because most of the survey work we do is in the winter. Most of our sites are grouse moors. Even the ones that aren't we still can't go on in bird nesting season, so that takes out April to June. We've got a window in July when we try and get surveys done, and then we can't get on the moors as often over the shooting season which is August sometimes up to December.

You come down out of the hill fog up there, and the Dales open out – you can see so far. It's good to have that space; not seeing people sometimes is quite nice! I live in Leeds in one of the back to back terraces and my view's of other people's houses, so I like being out on the moors.

I suppose I do look at landscapes differently now – I can't help it: I see the peat! I probably bore my friends with it, but I'm always saying 'I've worked there' or 'I've surveyed that hill'. There's nothing there as far as some people are concerned, but we get to see it in detail; we get to see all the plants that are there, and all the birdlife that comes back in February/March time. We do get views that a lot of people don't see because they tend to stick to footpaths further down, though this moorland is open access. We also get to see all the damaged blanket bog as well, which again lots of people won't have seen, because it's often right up on the tops, away from the footpaths.

Peatlands are an important habitat that store huge amounts of carbon when they aren't degrading. Globally, they contain twice as much carbon as the world's forests. Restoring damaged bogs can also improve water quality, protect archaeology and preserve a landscape that lots of people enjoy visiting.

Peat is formed from partially decomposed plant material and it can hold a lot of water. It's mainly made up of sphagnum mosses, which grow on the bogs. As the moss dies it doesn't rot away properly because of the acidic and anaerobic conditions. There are different kinds of peat bog – such as lowland raised bogs and the blanket peat, which tends to be on the tops and is fed only by the rain. Blanket bogs are a globally rare habitat and only about 4% of what we have in the UK is undamaged, for reasons such as drainage, overgrazing, fires, or peat cutting. Much of that damage is historic, but it takes so long for peat to recover: about ten years for a centimetre of peat to form, and it can be cut or burnt or drained really quickly.

Manmade drains called grips were cut into peat in the past; it was government funded and was mainly to try and drain the land for agricultural improvement, but they're just eroding and washing peat away.

My job is to go out and do the work on the ground: so doing the surveys of sites, writing restoration plans and then overseeing the restoration and revegetation work itself. On site we block up the manmade drains with peat dams and use timber sediment traps in the more natural-looking gullies. The dams and sediment traps are designed to slow the water down enough to let the peat sediment settle out. The idea is that it'll stabilise enough to let plants like sphagnum mosses and cotton grasses establish behind the dams and it will eventually, hopefully, re-vegetate completely. They're working very quickly in some places and the pools that have built up behind them are already filling with either cotton grasses or sphagnum, which is exactly what we want to happen.

Jan Hicks

Textile Artist and Smallholder

This is up on Orton Scar, with the Howgills in the distance. It's a view that I know well because I walk there a lot with the dogs. One of the things I really like to do on a summer's evening is go up there. During the day I don't get a lot of spare time, but in the evenings you can walk up there, take your sandwiches, sit and eat your tea and look at the view – it's just fabulous.

It doesn't show so well here because you're higher up, but looking at the Howgills from lower down, you get these rounded shapes in the hills. Wainwright referred to them as sleeping elephants, because they all sort of curl around each other.

We've been here 20 years. We just loved it here and so moved up from Oxford. As walkers, and rural people, we ended up with this place with ten acres. You've got to keep the land in condition. You can't just have ten acres of land and leave it, so we got some sheep. Initially we just had them as lawnmowers, but then I got into keeping the Angora goats. I've always knitted, and done textile stuff. I got the goats and then I got into the rare breed sheep, mainly Manx Laoghtans and Gotlands, which I keep for their fleece.

I've only got about 20 ewes at the moment. It's just a matter of checking them every day, feeding them during the winter, and routine maintenance, like doing their feet and worming them. And then you get periods of really intense activity, like lambing and clipping, and hay time. I love it; I can't imagine getting up in the morning and not having to go outside, even if it's only for half an hour to go round and feed and check everything.

I produce knitting yarn. I'd always done knitting, and it's great to be able to use your own wool, to make things from something you've known since you lambed it. I send the wool down to a company in Cornwall that does small scale spinning. I tend to dye the wools landscape colours, because they're the colours I'm comfortable with. I mix my own colours and do all my own dying. I sell the yarn and use some of it. I'm also an artist – textile art, felt

and wall hangings – and most of my stuff is based on landscape colours and landscape views. I belong to a women's co-operative which has a shop over in Caldbeck called The Wool Clip, so I have a good outlet for knitting yarn and kits for people to knit jumpers and socks and scarves.

In 2005 I did a piece with a friend who's also an artist. I've always loved the Uffington White Horse down in Berkshire. Of course there's no chalk here, but I got talking to this friend and we decided that we'd do our own and that we'd do it in fleece. We got 500 Swaledale fleeces up onto Wild Boar Fell, half way up, and did a wild boar in fleece. It was 300 feet long and 120 feet high and was there for about three weeks. It was a fantastic thing, and an amazing thing to do. It was quite interesting getting it up there, and getting it back down again!

Once you've got into keeping animals, you start learning to do the things like drystone walling, and just keeping the place up. You just learn as you go along, with help from the locals – who think you're completely barmy. I do have a principle that if something needs doing I like to be able to do it myself, so I clip all my own sheep, and I do my own walling. It's a really nice community round here. People will always do something for you, there's a lot of barter, and trading labour. If you need something done that you can't do yourself, someone will always do it, and you just help them out some other time. Haytime – there's three of us who have very small bits of land, and a bigger farm up the road. Everybody just mucks in, because he doesn't have the labour to get all his hay in, and we haven't got the machinery, so we all just help each other. And if you run out of hay or straw in the winter, somebody will always find you a few bales of hay, and then you help them out when they're stuck. It works really well. It's a real traditional sort of community.

Martin Davies

Countryside Property Manager, National Trust

This is the view looking up the valley from Moor End. I chose it because it gives a great view of a 'classic' U-shaped glaciated valley: moorland on the fell tops, steep valley side woodlands and the River Wharfe flowing through what is very much a working living landscape, rich in wildlife.

I'm responsible for the overall management of all the land in National Trust ownership within the Dales, which includes Upper Wharfedale, Malham Tarn Estate, and Braithwaite Hall etc. Our ownership stretches over 20,000 acres, but it is spread over a large geographic area and is very diverse. You've got this bleak and open landscape on Malham Moor, and then you go to Wharfedale which forms a slightly softer and more intimate landscape in comparison. We have some really stunning hay meadows, extensive areas of limestone pavement, steep gill and valley side woodland, tarns and wetlands, blanket peat habitat and several small mansion properties – a wide range of interesting places.

We look at the management of our land and how it contributes to the wider landscape – we are often trying to unpick past management which was promoted after the Second World War to try and improve food production and become more self sufficient. This included the large-scale drainage of moorland peat; reduction in native woodland cover; the loss of many flower-rich meadows; hard engineering of rivers and increases in livestock numbers.

These changes in some instances have had a major impact on the hydrology of many upland river systems. The drainage ditches in the peat (the peat acts as a natural sponge and releases water slowly) have increased the speed and amount of water feeding into the steep gills that drain the moor tops, which is then causing erosion of the gills. This brings high volumes of water and gravel into the main river system, which increases the height of the river bed. There has been work in the past to build up the banks to stop the river breaking out and flooding. What's actually happened in places is that they've built up the banks that much, the river's higher now than the rest of the flood plain, so it actually wants to break out and do something quite dramatic. But of course the flat valley floor is the most important bit for the farmers: that's where they produce the hay and the silage, which feeds the stock in the winter.

It's quite a challenge; the river is trying to re-naturalise itself and the National Trust aims to work as much as possible to allow natural processes to take place. However, the farming community would like to keep the flood plain protected as it is. It's about reaching that balance and working closely with our farm tenants to start the process of allowing the river to slowly naturalise, and giving time for the farmers to adapt their farming practices as the river changes. It's quite complex.

We've been working in partnership with other bodies and our farm tenants over the years. This work has included blocking up of drainage ditches (grips) on peat habitats; restoration and new planting of both gill and valley side woodlands; a series of soft-engineered river bank repairs, and flower-rich hay meadow restoration. This is all to help improve the hydrological function and wildlife diversity of Upper Wharfedale.

I personally love walking, mountain biking and kayaking. I feel very privileged to both work and play in such a special place and feel it gives you much more of an insight into how much everyone involved puts in to managing the Dales.

Dave Higgins

Project Manager, Yorkshire Dales Rivers Trust

The River Cover goes down the bottom of the valley here: you can see where it is from the line of trees. Coverdale's not a well visited dale, but it's lovely when you get down to the river. There's a real nice habitat mosaic there. You've got a lot of trees and woodland along the river bank, and the river looks just how you expect a river to look: a nice mix of gravels – with very little fine sediment, which is important – but there's also woody debris in there. In terms of fish, you've got your salmon, brown trout, probably sea trout, bullhead, stone loach, minnows, and native crayfish.

We've had the Coverdale Biodiversity Project going on up there for the last two years now, which involves the large-scale management of the riverscape. What we're doing there is looking at the catchment (which is the area that drains into that particular watershed), and using models such as SCIMAP (a fine sediment model) to work out where water flows, and possible diffuse pollution sources (small pockets of pollution with lots of them spread across a catchment). We then use restoration methods such as willow spiling, bank protection or gill planting.

Willow spiling is a fantastic way to spend a couple of days. We use fence posts up here rather than willow rods, just because of the nature of the bedrock and the gravel. You knock fence posts into the river bed, and then you have three or four metre willow rods which you just weave in and out to make one long hurdle. You angle it in at the upstream end of the bank, so it deflects the water around it and this protects the bank. It makes a permeable barrier, so it slows the water down and as it passes through the willows it allows fine sediments to deposit out behind the hurdle. This is a restoration method for places where you're getting quite a lot of severe erosion.

Coming up onto this hill we've got the Yorkshire Peat Partnership working on the top to block the grips and restore the peat soils, then we're working down in the bottom, and you've got the National Trust working in between.

Coverdale is a landscape with a lot of variety: you start off on these moorland plateaus and then work down on to the hill slopes, and then find yourself in these little valleys, and all the way you can walk from top to bottom, finding little out-of-the-way waterfalls and lovely little streams. But I think it's the character of the people who live here as well. Until this job I'd never really mixed with farmers, or lived in a rural community, but it's one hell of an experience. They're all approachable, they're all friendly. It's the whole mix, and each dale has its own uniqueness.

I was brought up in Hull, which is quite urban, with rivers you probably wouldn't want to go paddling in! My mum used to bring us on walking holidays up in the Dales. I've always been interested in natural history; I played rugby at school, and I think I was the only one in the team who would go and spend Saturday night owl-spotting!

This is a great job, especially when you're outdoors and wading in rivers, catching all the fish and insects and seeing what lives there. I used to go to places like Grassington, sit on an eroded bank side and just enjoy watching the river. But now you look at that bank and think 'that's eroded' and you need to do something. You look at the landscape in a completely different way. That's great in one way, but it also means that you're going around looking at negative things, thinking 'how can I improve that?', rather than just looking at it – because it is a beautiful landscape.

Roger Gaynor

Dales Volunteer, Yorkshire Dales National Park Authority

This is taken from the summit of Addlebrough, looking right into Wensleydale towards Hawes. I think it's the best viewpoint in the Dales. Addlebrough's got this beautiful shape. Here, you can just see the rim of limestone that goes all round the top of what's really Wensleydale's own Table Mountain. You stand there and it's like opening up 360 pages of a story book of the Dales: you can see where the Ice Age has carved out the dale; there is a deep feeling of ancient history with carved stones and a burial cairn at the summit; it was said to be a lookout station during Roman times; and then you get the stone walls as well.

I think you have to walk to the summit of Addlebrough to really appreciate Wensleydale. For me it's the most majestic dale because it's got this flat base. You can be within it and not really know you're in a dale, but once you get higher up you can see how wide it is, with the fells sort of keeping it together. It's fantastic.

I became a Dales Volunteer in 2005. I was approaching retirement and I thought, 'I've got to do something to keep me interested as I go along'. I've spent a lifetime managing trees and woodlands, so you could say this is a busman's holiday really!

The first year was a training and induction programme, which was really high quality. The staff here are all so committed and skilled and knowledgeable. I thought I knew something about the Dales before I came for the interview. I realise now that I was only scratching the surface. I'm still learning all the time, so it's been a great opportunity for me. I've learnt to read the landscape much better. In 2005 I could have stood at the top of Addlebrough and still enjoyed the view, but now when I'm at the top of somewhere like Addlebrough, I think, 'how was that valley formed? Was it a glacier, was it meltwater? Why are the fields that way? Why are these mounds here? Are they Iron Age settlements?'

Volunteers do a vast range of duties. We're looking at the very fabric of the Dales – the wildlife and the structure of the landscape as well. You really feel as though you're doing a worthwhile job.

I'm really keen on the Park's education and outreach programmes. They're so important in passing the National Park message on to future generations. On a very regular basis I, along with other volunteers and staff, take school groups and other groups out into the Park. It might just be for a general walk, or more specific to field work they're doing. I love that kind of work.

Whether we're working in a woodland, or on a footpath, or building a bridge somewhere, we're often approached by local people. It gives us an opportunity to strengthen links with local people, and get to know what's important to them. The visitors are important and help support the local economy, but the people who live here are really important; it's very much the landowners and farmers who keep this view here from Addlebrough.

I'm out there on a regular basis repairing footpaths, restoring the habitats and so on. I sometimes look at views like this and think, 'this is quite a rugged and, in a way, a fairly wild landscape, and yet here we are doing all this work to protect and conserve it'. So it's not really that rugged, not that wild perhaps – it is actually quite a fragile landscape and that's why we're doing this work. Looking at this view you know that without all the different organisations and all the different people involved in caring for that view it would suffer, and the harm that's caused would take years and years to put right – in fact some of it probably could never be put right. So whilst it's a rugged landscape it's still very fragile and really sensitive to change.

Sarah Butler

Writer

Our grandparents moved to Grassington when I was six and it has been a home from home for our whole family ever since. We are all keen walkers and I have many happy memories of walking in the area. This is a view from one of my favourite walks, from Grassington along High Lane, through the old hospital site and back along Edge Lane. It is taken from the footpath between Edge Lane and High Lane, looking over the valley to Barden Moor. I love the patterns of the drystone walls, and the two knolls which were once coral reefs.

I write and think a lot about place and what it is that makes us feel like we belong to a particular area. For me, people are as important in that equation as any aesthetic feature. *Working the View* has opened my eyes to just how many people are involved in caring for the Yorkshire Dales National Park. I can now look at a landscape which I've been walking in for years and see the evidence of that attention and work, in the walls and the fences, the animals, the paths, the peat, the rivers, and much more.

I conducted the interviews for *Working the View* over a period of eighteen months. Mark would meet me off the train from London with a carefully worked out itinerary, an envelope stuffed with maps, and keys for the hire car, and I would head off into the hills. I visited farms, offices and people's homes, often driving miles across the moors without seeing another person. After the bustle and hurry of London life it was a genuine treat, an experience which has taken me to new areas of the Dales and deepened my own connection to the area. I would return to the city not only armed with stories about sheep farming, peat restoration, water management, and the intricacies of propagating juniper, but also with that lightness and serenity that the Dales offers its visitors.

It has been an immense privilege to speak to people who are passionate about this part of the world, and whose day-to-day existence is bound up with the landscape in a whole range of different ways. Many times I've sat listening to someone explain what it is that makes the Yorkshire Dales National Park special and have been struck by the poetry of their language. I have kept each text in the book in the words of the participant, merely editing and reordering to make a coherent 'piece', because I wanted to capture these different voices and the passion behind the words.

I hope that reading these stories will add an extra dimension to Mark's beautiful photographs, and offer a unique insight into the people involved in helping sustain this very special landscape.

Mark Butler

Photographer

This project has been a great experience for me, it has offered a change of perspective in the way I work. Previously I would go out looking for locations I think will 'work', based on the conditions/season/weather in which I found them. For this project I was provided with the locations, so I needed to think much more how to make them work as images, when they would look at their best, the direction of the light, and so on.

Most locations were provided as written descriptions, so the first stage was to visit these spots. Whilst there I would look for foreground interest to provide depth to the image, work out a good composition, decide what sun direction would make the image work best and therefore what time of day and season I needed to try to take the photograph. Other considerations were whether the image would look best when the heather was out, trees were in leaf or bare, or when snow was on the ground. Once I had my time frame, I then kept a very close eye on the weather to identify times when the conditions would be favourable for taking photographs. I didn't always get it right, but when I did, it was a magical experience.

There is something about being out and about at dawn which it is hard to describe. The struggle out of bed, driving to and climbing up to the location, whilst an effort, don't seem too bad once you've managed the initial push into consciousness, and there is always the excitement of seeing the sun rise to spur you on. For me there is always the panic that I'll get there too late, sometimes justified if I haven't allowed enough time, but mostly just because it gets lighter earlier than I expect it to. After the rush to get to the location and set up, there is then usually plenty of time to stand back, admire the view and the effects of the ever-changing weather and light upon it. I have spent many a happy hour in these locations just watching the scene change until I decided the time was right to capture the image.

Photographing these locations has often been a challenge. It can be hard to take a viewpoint which holds personal memories and experiences for the participant and turn it into an image which will be appealing for someone without those same associations. The problem can be that whilst you stand and observe a view, you take in the whole panorama and your experience includes elements which cannot be captured in a picture: the wind against your face, the sounds and smells around you. David Butterworth's comment that no matter how good a photographer is, they can't capture the essence of the place is very true. I can only capture a section of the landscape at a moment in time and in the way I view it. Only by visiting these locations will you get the true experience which the participants describe in the accompanying texts.

When you know the Dales as well as I do, it is very hard to pick a single favourite view. I have a soft spot for the Grassington viewpoint chosen by Sarah (for the same reasons), for the Littondale view chosen by Roger Gibson (memories of walking in the area), and now a great number of the viewpoints featured in this book (for the memories of capturing them), but I have chosen a view in Swaledale here. For this project I was based just outside the southern edge of the National Park, an hour and a half drive from Swaledale. Though I visit the area less regularly than other parts of the Park, I always look forward to going there, and it always seems like a holiday when I do.

This project has been a great opportunity for me to discover new viewpoints and see dawn or dusk through the seasons. I have discovered a wealth of fantastic locations and have enjoyed every outing. I hope my images have done some justice to the fantastic landscapes to be found in the Yorkshire Dales National Park and hope they inspire you to go out and experience them for yourselves.

Photographic Credits

All landscape photography is by Mark Butler, most portrait photography is by Sarah Butler. A number of portraits were provided by the participants and where the copyright holder is known and would like crediting, their details are below:

Jane Le Cocq portrait © Sam Le Cocq
Alistair Nash portrait © Louise Higgins
David Butterworth portrait © YDNPA
Gary Lodge portrait © Rebecca Le Cocq
Mark Butler portrait © Jim Round

Acknowledgements

Most of all we would like to thank all the participants featured in this book who have given up their time and shared their stories with us. It has been an honour to work with you all.

Mark would like to thank his wife Em for her help and support throughout the project, including carrying his equipment up hills at dawn or dusk, and making tea and breakfast at the top.

Thanks to all the proof readers (and sorry if you still disagree with our punctuation!!), and to the Arts Council who funded the project work.

Both of us would like to thank our parents, Anne and Dave, who taught us to follow our dreams...

Barden Moor at dawn

Because we have had to condense the interviews to make them fit into this book, any errors or omissions are most likely the fault of the authors (or due to disagreements between the proof readers on the use of punctuation - Mark personally, hopes to never have to use a semi-colon again!)

Visit the project website at: **www.workingtheview.co.uk**